Facilitating Preschool Literacy

Robin Campbell, Editor
University of Hertfordshire
Watford, United Kingdom

International Reading Association
800 Barksdale Road, PO Box 8139
Newark, Delaware 19714-8139, USA
www.reading.org

The International Reading Association attempts, through its publications, to provide a forum for a wide spectrum of opinions on reading. This policy permits divergent viewpoints without implying the endorsement of the Association.

Director of Publications   Joan M. Irwin
Managing Editor, Books and Electronic Publications   Christian A. Kempers
Associate Editor   Matthew W. Baker
Assistant Editor   Janet S. Parrack
Assistant Editor   Mara P. Gorman
Publications Coordinator   Beth Doughty
Association Editor   David K. Roberts
Production Department Manager   Iona Sauscermen
Graphic Design Coordinator   Boni Nash
Electronic Publishing Supervisor   Wendy A. Mazur
Electronic Publishing Specialist   Anette Schütz-Ruff
Electronic Publishing Specialist   Cheryl J. Strum
Electronic Publishing Assistant   Peggy Mason

Library of Congress Cataloging in Publication Data
    Facilitating preschool literacy / Robin Campbell, editor.
      p.   cm.
    Includes bibliographical references and index.
     1. Language arts (Preschool)   2. Reading (Preschool)   3. Early childhood education—Parent participation.   I. Campbell, Robin, 1937–   . II. International Reading Association.
LB1140.5.L3F33   1998   98-10386
372.6—dc21
ISBN 0-87207-187-1

Contents

Foreword

THIS BOOK PAINTS FOR THE READER A COLORFUL PICTURE OF the energetic lives of preschool children and their teachers. It enabled me to recapture the days when I, as a teacher of young children, tried desperately to reflect on the significance of children's literacy experiences while I was cleaning out the hamster cage. In *Facilitating Preschool Literacy* the reader finds lively glimpses of young children as they pretend to burn sausages, play monster games, and dress up and tell one another stories. But the authors of these chapters go beyond reminding us of the importance of play to describe the complexity of early-literacy experiences and the roles of teachers and parents in engaging children in the world of books and print.

The writers remind us that young children strive to make sense of their worlds through many kinds of representation: play, talk, drawing and writing, and in shared experiences with literature. The book includes rich descriptions of teachable moments seized upon, and connections between home and school gently nurtured into partnerships. There are frequent examples of teachers and parents listening respectfully to preschoolers in their search to understand how language and literacy emerge in the lives of young children.

This book contains detailed descriptions of language and literacy interactions in a wide variety of early-childhood settings in the United Kingdom, the United States, and Australia. The international scope of *Facilitating Preschool Literacy* represents an important emphasis for the International Reading Association, whose members are increasingly concerned with language and literacy issues in diverse settings. In reading this book you will be joining, in spirit at least, and international network of teacher-researchers who share a dedication to classroom-based research. Each chapter represents many hours of careful observation and reflection, a distillation of thousands of teaching encounters on three continents.

Another international trend is the current preoccupation with "balance" in reading and language-arts programs. This concern is echoed in this book, but here balance is exemplified in literacy programs in which creativity and intellectual challenge are intertwined. We are reminded in a gentle way that focus on children's interests and needs does not preclude intense informal literacy experiences. The "lifelong learner" so beloved by educational policymakers truly begins in the classrooms described in these pages.

Congratulations to the contributors to *Facilitating Preschool Literacy*, who have warmly invited readers into their early-childhood classrooms around the world.

Angela Ward
University of Saskatchewan
Saskatoon, Saskatchewan, Canada

Contributors

Jo Ann Brewer
Associate Professor
Salem State College
Salem, Massachusetts, USA

Robin Campbell
Professor of Primary Education
University of Hertfordshire
Hertfordshire, United Kingdom

Ruby E. Campbell
Early Years Teacher
Marks Gate Infants School
Barking, United Kingdom

Nigel Hall
Reader in Literacy Education
Didsbury School of Education
Manchester Metropolitan University
Manchester, United Kingdom

Prisca Martens
Assistant Professor of Language Education
Indiana University, Indianapolis
Indianapolis, Indiana, USA

Linda Miller
Principal Lecturer in Early Years Education
University of Hertfordshire
Hertfordshire, United Kingdom

Gretchen Owocki
Assistant Professor
Saginaw Valley State University
University Center, Michigan, USA

Bronwyn Reynolds
Early Childhood Educator/Literacy Consultant
Eltham College
Eltham, Victoria, Australia

Gill Scrivens
Senior Lecturer (Early Years)
University of Hertfordshire
Hertfordshire, United Kingdom

Patricia G. Smith
Deputy Director, Assessment Research Centre
Royal Melbourne Institute of Technology
Bundoora, Victoria, Australia

Julie Spreadbury
Professor of Language and Literacy Education
Queensland University of Technology
Red Hill, Australia

Diane A. Walworth
Title 1 Coordinator
Chenowith School District
The Dalles, Oregon, USA

Jo Weinberger
Lecturer in Education
University of Sheffield
Sheffield, United Kingdom

Introduction

Robin Campbell

As LITERACY RESEARCH HAS DEVELOPED IN RECENT YEARS THREE
important strands have become apparent in relation to the preschool child.
First, there is the perception of children as active constructors of their own
learning. Second, there is the recognition of the support that families provide in the early literacy learning of children. Third, there is an acceptance
that preschool settings have to reflect the literacy learning that occurs in
many homes and must provide opportunities for children to further develop their literacy. Each of these themes is important for preschool educators to consider, and I will comment on each in this Introduction.

Intensive case studies of young children developing as readers and
writers (for example, Bissex, 1980; Schickedanz, 1990) have demonstrated how children construct their own understanding of reading and
writing. Reading and writing initially may be unconventional with mis-
cues in the reading alongside scribbles and invented, or developmental,
spellings in their writing. Nevertheless, children's progress is evident during literacy activities as they increase their understandings about written
language systems (Goodman, 1990; Kamii, Manning, & Manning, 1991).
An acceptance of the views presented in these studies has a profound influence on the way early-years educators provide learning opportunities
for the children in their care. The emphasis should be on provision,

support, guidance, and the facilitation of learning. This creates a nontraditional view of the nature of teaching with young children.

Teachers recognize the very important role that families provide in encouraging the literacy development of their children. Edmund Huey (1908/1972) suggested of reading development that "The secret of success lies in parents' reading aloud to and with the child" (p. 332). Teachers may have lost sight of this dictum for a period, but it is now fully in the mainstream of educational thinking. For instance, Taylor and Strickland (1986) detailed accounts of parents sharing storybooks with their children. The accounts demonstrated the benefits to children from such sharings and also indicated the variety of family backgrounds within which storybook reading can take place.

Although storybook reading has such an important place in supporting children's reading development, there are many other literacy activities taking place in the home that support literacy (Weinberger, 1996). It is useful to be reminded of the many opportunities presented by newspapers, magazines, and comics; letters, bills, and shopping lists; and, of course, television. However, it is not the materials alone that encourage children toward literacy. The role of the parent or caregiver who supports the child is important. Geekie and Raban (1993) noted the positive support and encouragement that often is provided at home, especially by mothers. They also suggested that schools need to provide interactions between the teacher and children that approximates more closely to the earlier positive interactions between mother and child. This is not always easily achieved in classrooms, especially those in which the class size might be large. Nevertheless, it is useful to be reminded of the important role of the adult in the preschool setting; he or she, through interaction with the child, can do much to facilitate literacy learning.

The preschool educator will want to build on and continue to link with the home literacy provision that already has been established by the parent or caregiver. Of course, story reading will form part of the preschool activities. And although the larger groupings for story readings will alter the nature of the interactions, the readings in many preschools will remain interactive as the teacher encourages the children to comment and question, and therefore to become partners in the activity (Dombey, 1988). Typically preschools use play as a central part of the day.

However, opportunities for play can be organized by the adult to ensure that there are reading and writing possibilities for the children (Hall & Abbott, 1991). Literacy activities are extended and include nursery rhymes, songs, use of environmental print, opportunities for writing, shared book experience, and shared reading (Campbell, 1996). However, as the authors in this text emphasize, literacy activities are used for the children to construct their own meanings; direct teaching should have a more limited role.

This book has been organized to reflect the three themes offered at the beginning of this Introduction. There are contributions from both academic university staff with a commitment to early-years education, and from classroom teachers of preschool children. Therefore, both theoretical and practical perspectives are presented; it is important that both sets of perspectives are available for the reader. Additionally, the contributions come from three English-speaking communities—Australia, the United Kingdom, and the United States. So, there is an international perspective to the text, offered in a range of voices and styles. This international perspective requires some background on the organizational structures for preschool education that apply in each of these countries.

Preschool Education in Australia, the United Kingdom, and the United States

The preschool provision in Australia has altered since the introduction of the Child Care Act of 1972 and the subsequent development of a Children's Services Program. Any funding now is likely to come from the state governments, but there is also an element of payment by the family. The preschools now cater to 4-year-old children in the year before they enter kindergarten.

In Australia, there are many types of programs other than preschool. These include day nurseries, neighborhood centers, private day care, franchised day care, and integrated preschool day care that provides both a sessional preschool program and a day-care service and work-based day care. The regulations prescribed to control child care aim to protect the safety, health, education, and welfare of children who enter a program. The educational aspect, therefore, is only one part of the provision.

Programs in Australian preschools are developed as a result of pre-service training and informal apprenticeship. Most preservice students expect to find jobs in child care rather than as preschool teachers. The programs are based around indoor and outdoor play activities with a focus on making them developmentally appropriate. Invitations to write or to build on the children's experiences in a print-filled environment are provided by only a few knowledgeable practitioners.

In the United Kingdom children begin formal schooling at 5 years of age when they enter the reception class of an infant school. However, some districts have the entrance date as early as the September of the academic year in which the child reaches 5. Therefore, some children enter a reception class shortly after their fourth birthday, and they will be in a class of perhaps 30 children with just one teacher. For most 3- and 4-year-olds, however, the provision of a preschool will come in a variety of formats. First, there will be nursery classrooms attached to a state or independent school, or to free-standing nursery schools. There the children usually are taught by a qualified teacher supported often by a nursery nurse (with a 2-year full-time qualification acquired after 16 years of age) with a ratio of one adult to 13 children. Second, there is the private play group provision, often led by a nursery nurse, where the children will have more adult support of perhaps one adult to five to eight children. Typically these play groups are found in village halls, community centers, and church halls. Third, there are the day-care nurseries where the children may be in baby classes from the time they reach 6 months of age, toddler classes up to about 2 years of age, and then nursery classes for 3- and 4-year-olds. This variety of provision has been subject to educational inspection that includes, for the 4-year-olds, an inspection of the learning opportunities in language and literacy. In all of these settings any emphasis on literacy is informal with story reading being a central part of the provision. Children are likely to have the opportunity to recognize and write their own name and there are alphabet charts in the room. Some classrooms will offer far more than this, however, and those settings are described in the chapters describing learning environments in the United Kingdom.

It is difficult to describe a typical experience for preschool children in the United States because the school settings may vary from state to state. However, all children begin kindergarten if they are 5 years old before September 1 of the academic year. For 4-year-old children there are nursery school or preschool programs in a number of states. There also are public programs for children with disabilities at age 3. The teachers in the public-school programs must hold a certificate issued by their state and are required to have a bachelor's degree with specific courses completed in early childhood education. There is a wide variety of requirements for teachers outside the public school system. Most schools require a teacher-child ratio of 1:12 or 1:15 for classes of 3- or 4-year-olds. In these classes there also can be an assistant teacher whose highest level of schooling may be high school. In addition to the school classes there are also some child-care settings with minimal teaching requirements.

The programs for the children tend to fall into three main categories: academic, Montessori, and developmental programs. Some academic programs stress learning to read through formal instruction for children as young as 2. More developmentally oriented programs and Montessori programs usually engage children in informal literacy activities, but do not provide formal instruction until the children are in kindergarten or first grade. The majority of U.S. children begin formal literacy instruction in kindergarten.

This summary of the preschool provisions in the three countries inevitably is incomplete and does not do justice to the variety that will exist in each country. However, these descriptions do provide some background against which the various contributions in the three sections of this book can be read.

Organization of the Book

The first part and first chapter of the book consider the notion of children constructing literacy. In Chapter 1 Smith considers theories propounded by Chomsky, de Beaugrande, Piaget, Bruner, Halliday, and Vygotsky and provides a foundation for the subsequent chapters. She views children as theory builders and hypothesis testers who require experiences that challenge them as learners but that can be accomplished with sensitive adult guidance. These views are reflected subsequently in the chapters written by both academics and classroom teachers. Although

Chapter 1 leads in naturally to the rest of the text, many readers may return to it from time to time as the other more practical chapters are linked back to theory.

Part Two looks at literacy in the context of the family. Chapter 2 by Spreadbury emphasizes the widely recognized importance of story reading to young children at home. It is a transcript in which the reader can follow a mother reading with her 14-month-old son. During this reading aloud there also is discussion about the text and illustrations in the book. The child's literacy development is being facilitated by the adult with a storybook as the medium for the facilitation.

Weinberger's Chapter 3 extends our perception beyond the importance of story reading by looking at the wide range of literacy events that many children experience in the home before they move on to a preschool setting. The chapter is developed from the information collected about 3-year-old children, especially during the Elmswood project in Sheffield, England (Weinberger, 1996). The author indicates that children of all backgrounds experience authentic literacy encounters drawn from the real world. Story reading is an important part of home literacy provision and learning, but Weinberger emphasizes that there are numerous other activities in the home that facilitate children's literacy learning.

In Chapter 4 Martens looks at one child's development as a reader and writer. We meet Sarah, ages 2 to 5, and experience with her how she grows as a reader and writer in the context of her home and family environment. We examine how Sarah generates questions for herself about literacy. Questions that frame her inquiry ask how and why reading and writing function for her personally in our society and how she can participate as a reader and writer in her community. Sarah's questions "What are you doing with that written language?" "How can I read and write?" and "How do we read and write?" are not conscious questions she can voice. Nevertheless we see evidence of them driving her learning as she invents hypotheses about how to read and write. She does so using the knowledge she has and continually refines her understandings as she becomes more experienced with literacy.

Part Three is the largest part of this book. It takes us from the theory and the home background to look more directly at literacy learning in preschool settings. In Chapter 5 I provide an overview of the literacy activities and the role of the teacher in the preschool. This exploration is based on observations of teachers at work with 3- and 4-year-old children in preschool classrooms (Campbell, 1996). The key use of story readings is noted, and the development from that activity to shared book experience and shared reading is also considered. Throughout the chapter there is evidence of children at play with literacy and learning literacy in the process. There are also constant reminders of the teacher as a provider, demonstrator, support, guide, and facilitator for the children in this literacy learning.

An area untouched in Chapter 5 is that of the child as a storyteller. This topic is discussed by Hall in Chapter 6, in which he reminds us that storytelling is an act of authorship and that it can be encouraged in preschool settings. He then describes three ways in which the teacher can create opportunities for children to function as storytellers. For each of the activities of self-recorded stories, adult-recorded stories, and symbolic play as storytelling, examples are provided from the children themselves. The chapter is a powerful argument to support the view that teachers need to provide space and opportunity for children's storytelling as part of their literacy development.

Miller follows with Chapter 7 which is devoted to the importance of environmental print. The chapter looks at the way some preschool settings link with parents to explore the print that surrounds most, if not all, children. The study of parents and 3-year-old children exploring environmental print provides some interesting examples of children trying to make sense of the print around them. It also emphasizes the key role of the adult in responding to the children's questions about print.

Many teachers are now faced with the challenge of supporting children from a variety of linguistic backgrounds. Brewer provides an example from the United States in Chapter 8, which demonstrates the similarities and differences of working in trilingual settings. First, it is evident that the role of adults, a print-rich environment, and the use of play with literacy contexts are all important in this type of classroom just like other preschool settings. However, the adults also ensure that each of the three languages (English, Spanish, and Khmer) are valued and that each child has the opportunity to use them.

The first of three chapters written by classroom teachers is provided in Chapter 9 by Campbell. Her example from a classroom in East London emphasizes the use of story reading not only for the story itself, but as a means of generating other activities in the classroom. The author shows how the children's contributions can be used to construct a Big Book and therefore can lead to their own books being available for future story readings. The story and the story reading can create the curriculum in the classroom.

Walworth's Chapter 10 tells about establishing an alternative kindergarten for literacy learning. She reminds the reader about the difficulties of making a change in any school and shows how changes toward a more holistic, child-centered preschool class where literacy is encouraged can occur. This chapter also links an outline program from Australia with observations of nursery provision in the United Kingdom to the developments in a U.S. classroom.

Chapter 11 by Reynolds explores the author's development from a preschool teacher placing little emphasis on literacy to one for whom literacy became central in the classroom. She discusses the important role of the teacher, the transformation of the classroom into a rich literacy environment, and the use of stories—for reading and as the basis for the preschool curriculum. Whereas Chapter 9 provides considerable detail of the use of one story in a preschool class, this chapter complements that analysis by exploring more widely a range of books that support the children in various ways.

Scrivens looks more broadly at nursery children as readers and writers in Chapter 12. She draws from her experience as a nursery teacher and as a university tutor to look in detail at the literacy development of six children in a preschool. Her study uses the observed reading and writing behavior of the children to inform us of their literacy development. However, she also adds the children's comments about reading and writing, which demonstrate them actively constructing views about the process of reading as they explore literacy in their preschool classroom.

Finally, in Chapter 13 Owocki returns us to a fundamental feature of preschools, namely the important role of play in children's learning. The author begins by demonstrating the careful planning that is required of the play environment so that literacy opportunities are enhanced, then presents details of the support that teachers provide in facilitating literacy during the play. This final chapter serves as a reminder of the totality of the book. It shows the child as an active constructor of literacy learning and reminds the reader of the diverse knowledge that children bring to their classroom. It also emphasizes one other feature—just as all the other chapters do— the important and sophisticated role of the teacher as a facilitator of children's literacy.

References

Bissex, G. (1980). *GNYS AT WRK: A child learns to read and write.* Cambridge, MA: Harvard University Press.

Campbell, R. (1996). *Literacy in nursery education.* Stoke-on-Trent, UK: Trentham Books.

Dombey, H. (1988). Partners in the telling. In M. Meek & C. Mills (Eds.), *Language and literacy in the primary school.* Lewes, UK: Falmer.

Geekie, P., & Raban, B. (1993). *Learning to read and write through classroom talk.* Stoke-on-Trent, UK: Trentham Books.

Goodman, Y. (Ed.). (1990). *How children construct literacy: Piagetian perspectives.* Newark, DE: International Reading Association.

Hall, N., & Abbott, L. (Eds.). (1991). *Play in the primary curriculum.* London: Hodder and Stoughton.

Huey, E. (1908/1972). *The psychology and pedagogy of reading.* Cambridge, MA: Massachusetts Institute of Technology Press.

Kamii, C., Manning, M., & Manning, G. (Eds.). (1991). *Early literacy: A constructivist foundation for whole language.* Washington, DC: National Education Association.

Schickedanz, J.A. (1990). *Adam's righting revolutions.* Portsmouth, NH: Heinemann.

Taylor, D., & Strickland, D. (1986). *Family storybook reading.* New York: Scholastic.

Weinberger, J. (1996). *Literacy goes to school.* London: Paul Chapman.

Part One

Children Constructing Literacy

1

Coming to Know One's World: Development as Social Construction of Meaning

Patricia G. Smith

THE TERM SOCIAL CONSTRUCTIVISM IS VERY FAMILIAR THROUGH ITS use in the literature that focuses on children's learning. Constructivist approaches have their roots in fields as seemingly diverse as linguistics, psychology, sociology, semiotics, and philosophy. Through a small exploration of the work of some scholars in these fields it is possible to trace the development of a view of knowledge as an active construction built by an individual. This individual acts within a social context that shapes and contains that knowledge, but goes on to create new meaning in the social world. The creation of this reality may be described as coming to know one's world. Each learner, child or philosopher, is able to use language to promote thought to explicate culture and to hold this new cultural history in mind. This theory of learning must underpin the experiences offered to students in early childhood classrooms.

Although there is strong support among the educational community for a constructive approach to children's learning, this approach often means different things to different people. Educators' ideas may come from their own experiences or from their acquaintance with the theoretical perspectives of learning. The way in which they interact with children, their expectations about children, and how they set up learning environments are indicators of educators' beliefs whether they realize it or not. An overview of the development of constructivist theories about teaching and learning will allow us to trace where certain beliefs and practices have originated so that teachers may make informed decisions about change in their preschool settings.

The Psychological Perspective of Language and Learning

Behavioral Models of Learning

It has been argued that Socrates is the first documented constructivist. The discussion in this chapter does not go back that far except to observe that since ancient Greek times, philosophy has been divided into two schools of thought about the nature of the human mind and how human beings acquire knowledge. The mechanistic view, which has dominated thought in the Western world since the 17th century, was developed by the French philosopher Descartes. He compared knowledge to a clock, a machine that could be understood by taking it apart and then reassembling it. Descartes (1637/1978) argued that some ideas are put into mind by God as innate knowledge. His view was challenged by the empiricism of the English philosopher John Locke (1690/1974), according to whom the mind at birth is a blank page, open to learning but not in any way directing the acquisition of knowledge.

Locke's view of the importance of experience in learning has been advanced particularly by American behavioral psychologists such as Skinner (1969), who similarly suggested that the learner was passive, subject to direction, and controlled by the surrounding world. Skinner argued that there are no limits to learning except the limits imposed by experience, through which knowledge is built slowly and cumulatively as successive desirable responses to stimuli are rewarded (positive reinforcement) and unwanted behaviors are punished (negative reinforcement).

Behavioral scientists described associationist models of language learning to account for language development. Their view of language learning was based largely on how classical languages had been studied.

They were concerned mainly with the description of language in terms of the classification and function of the words within it. They thought that children acquire language through imprinting and imitation; that they are passive receivers of language who should be directed toward an adult model through positive reinforcement of imitative behavior.

It was the linguist Chomsky (1965) who provided the first real challenge to the idea of language learning as imitative behavior and in doing so drew explicitly from the work of Descartes. According to Chomsky, language development is a matter of gaining facility with rules that govern language during childhood. Children are not taught to use the rules; instead, this ability matures spontaneously with exposure to the language environment. Chomsky emphasized that the process is more than pure imitation (a key concept in behaviorist theories), as could be seen by the child's production of new and interesting sentences.

This mature, adult grammar became the yardstick by which children's language development was assessed. As a result, perceptions of language learning remained largely product dominated, viewed in terms of what the child could or could not do relative to an adult product (the perfect grammar used by mature or adult speakers). It is not surprising, therefore, that notions of language deficit evolved to explain the failure of some learners to acquire a level of language that was in accord with the adult model. These notions are still popular today, for example, with educators who insist on perfect spelling or describe reading ability in age levels.

Because Chomsky's approach had provided little theory about how language development proceeds, there had been no link between inner predispositions and environmental factors. Instead the approach was what de Beaugrande (1980) would call a description of the virtual systems of language; these are systems of sounds, grammatical forms, and sentence structures available to a language user, but are not a complete description of what is used. In short, Chomsky's grammar focused on the sentence isolated from the linguistic content and the social context in which it occurs. As such, it had logical validity but not psychological validity.

The functional approach to language suggested by de Beaugrande is reflected in the work of others, including the cognitive learning theories of Piaget (1978), which are examined in the next section. Based on a view about the nature of language learning that held the human mind to be endowed at birth with certain predefining dispositions, there came about a wide acceptance of the position that children are active, rule-oriented beings who acquire much of their language on their own initiative. This view was supported by the evidence of everyday experience. A major theme was to be that language learners are theory builders and hypothesis testers.

Developmental Approaches to Language and Learning

Piaget's (1976) biologically based notion of cognitive growth also was developmental. This view of the importance of experience contrasted the behaviorist view that development results entirely from learning and that the child absorbs information as he or she develops. For Piaget, development was the dominant process; learning followed after it and structures already in place were refined and improved. He believed that children pass through several stages in the process of development. Because progression depends mainly on maturational factors, the child is unable to move to a higher stage until he or she is in command of the previous stage.

Learning occurs through the child's attempts to make sense of the world through exploration and manipulation. The internal control by the child results in learning, so it is not useful for adults to try to hasten the developmental process by telling the child how to do something. Language grows out of this activity and helps the child internalize the learning, but it does not *lead* the learning. It is always experience that does this.

Piaget believed that a crucial factor for development was conflict, which causes the learner to restructure existing knowledge. He described the human mind as a set of mental structures (schemata) that help people make sense of what they perceive. As a child matures and experiences the world, these structures grow, and new information is integrated into the thinking as the conflict caused by new experiences that challenge early beliefs is resolved into new learning. The temporary cognitive stability resulting from this balance of assimilation and accommodation is called *equilibrium.*

This rather simplistic discussion of Piaget's theory of assimilation, accommodation, fixed equilibrium, and a static stage theory of learning offers a view that underlies many preschool and school programs today. This has happened even though Piaget kept working to understand human development and in later years offered a model of dynamic equilibrium characterized by successive coordination and progressive equilibration.

Chomsky achieved a privileged position for transformational linguistics in academic disciplines. At the same time argumentative psychology, as typified by Piaget, also was claiming attention. This resulted in a unification of the two fields of study, which caused the emergence of the field of psycholinguistics. In particular, Chomsky identified the role of syntax, the rule-governed part of the language system that includes both grammar and morphology patterning and enables human beings, who all possess an innate predisposition to do so, to make sense of language. Piaget's concepts of assimilation and accommodation gave evidence of the learners' active involvement in learning language. These studies focused on static rather than dynamic language and on individual speakers rather than communities.

The Sociological Perspective of Language and Learning

Learning in Social Contexts

The view of constructivism suggesting that each individual constructs knowledge that is individual and unique to the learner has been challenged. Since the early 1980s much theory and research on human cognitive development have focused on the cultural and contextual basis of development. This line of research has resulted in increased attention to the social context in which learning occurs. This focus has occurred because of the paradox of the learner's using only individually constructed knowledge and the need to develop shared semiotics—the social knowledge, or meanings, of the culture.

Kuhn (1962) in his classic work *The Structure of Scientific Revolutions* argued that knowledge is not made through individual encounters with the physical world but exists because of negotiation by many individual knowers. Symbolic negotiation was a process in which competing propositions attempted to establish believable claims that had to fit with existing thought. Only when such a claim was established could a proposition be elevated to the status of knowledge.

The outcome of Piaget's theory of intellectual development was the belief that children would be allowed to do their own learning through experience. Kuhn used the term *paradigm* to describe the way perception and thinking are ordered. He used the term *paradigm shift* to refer to the process that takes place within someone who is willing and able to change a belief because new knowledge has been developed and the old belief is no longer possible. A paradigm shift had been required for those who believed that a child was a passive learner who would learn only by being told something. Another paradigm shift was required with the introduction of Vygotsky's theory that describes the cognitive process as shared between people.

Language as the Sociocultural Tool for Making Meaning

Since the early 1980s much work has been done to introduce the work of the Vygotsky to the Western world. Because Vygotsky was concerned with the social aspects of learning and knowledge and not just the cognitive or psychological aspects, he had some different views from Piaget and his followers. He used the metaphor of internalization to describe the basic process involved in learning—the passage of knowledge from culture to mind. He believed that all higher mental functions had social origins that always would be obvious to an observer. These appeared at first *between* individuals before they existed *within* the individual. However, this internalization does not involve producing an exact copy because the individual adapts the information and personalizes it.

Wertsch (1991), who has analyzed much of Vygotsky's work, noted the following:

> [Vygotsky] is not simply claiming that social interaction leads to the development of the child's abilities in problem solving, memory, etc.; rather he is saying that the very means (especially speech) used in social interaction are taken over by the individual child and internalized. Thus, Vygotsky is making a very strong statement here about internalization and the social foundations of cognition. (p. 145)

Because language helps the learner reflect on behavior, Vygotsky viewed it as the foundation for all cognitive processes, including self-awareness, concept formation, and problem solving. Vygotsky stressed the role of social communication in cognitive development by forming the theory that children's learning takes place within the Zone of Proximal

Development (ZPD). According to his research, tasks within the ZPD are too difficult to be done alone but can be accomplished through cooperative dialogue with adults or more skilled peers. Bruner (1986) also described this help as "taking a loan on consciousness" (p. 74) or "scaffolding" (p. 76). Children can take the language of these verbal instructions and make it part of their private speech to organize their own independent efforts in the same way. According to Vygotsky, it is through this process in each culture that cognitive skills required for success are transmitted socially from generation to generation.

This theory of learning can be designated a context-specific approach to cognition in which language is a socioculturally provided tool for the construction of thought.

Adherents of a sociological view of knowledge, following Vygotsky's concept of development, have perceived it as being a function of various kinds of social and cultural influences in the environment. Because language is a social phenomenon, encounters with language mean encounters with it as it is used in a particular culture. Heath (1982) has expressed this view as follows:

> A unilinear model of development in the acquisition of language structures cannot adequately account for culturally diverse ways of acquiring knowledge or developing cognitive styles. (p. 73)

Halliday (1975) suggested that children quickly become aware of language as communication and argued that young children use preverbal utterances to communicate. He also contended that language serves three abstract macrofunctions: The ideational function deals with information about the world and how different elements in the world relate to one another; the interpersonal function is concerned with how people relate to one another (what roles they play and what attitudes they bring to a situation); and the textual function looks at how the various elements of language function in relation to one another (how language is organized to give information and to establish and maintain social relationships). Halliday found that it was an awareness of the interpersonal functions of language that was acquired first. Thus, the sociological view saw development as determined by environment or by exposure to the appropriate demonstrations.

Toward a Synthesis of Psychological and Sociological Perspectives

It already has become obvious that to place theories of knowledge and learning into a dichotomous psychological and sociological framework is too artificial. It could be argued that until Vygotsky's work became known in the Western world the sociological view had ignored the distinction between modeling and learning; exposure did not automatically lead to learning. Also, the way in which individuals experience the social context differently had been understated. The sociological view regarded development as being the direct outcome of input received, whereas the psychological view implied a concept of development that was universal and ultimately was only affected indirectly by the social context.

A Semiotic Perspective Adds to Meaning Making

The problems led researchers to seek ways of synthesizing the psychological and sociological approaches. A semiotic perspective looks at areas where ideas about children's learning converge. Semiotics, which is about signs and codes and icons and meanings, is an example of a field of study that may be used to demonstrate a move from views that originated with Locke and Descartes. Locke claimed that human knowledge emerges through impact with the environment; a Cartesian line of reasoning views the human mind largely in terms of universal, innate categories and structures and views the environment largely in terms of how it provides testing of innately given hypotheses and how it influences developmental processes.

Early semioticians who followed Locke contributed toward a behaviorist notion of language acquisition. The structural linguist de Saussure (1916/1966) thought that semiotics could be viewed as a theory of communication. For example, a word is read or spoken and meaning is not in a word but is functional, the result of its difference from other words. The way an individual interprets the world is a function of the language he or she has available. According to this approach reality is not reflected by language but is produced by it.

Eco (1979) articulated a more active view of the language learner. According to his studies, semiotics is the study of everything that can be taken as a sign. Language is an example of a semiotic, or sign, system. If language is viewed from this perspective, then language learning becomes a matter of learning to recognize, interpret, and use this sign system. Because it is the members of a culture who determine signs and their meaning, language learning occurs through the interaction of the learner with members of the cultural group. As we have seen, Halliday (1978) also has argued for this semiotic view of the language learner.

Early in the 1930s Vygotsky (1934/1978) had already argued for the role of social experience in shaping and interpreting children's worlds. Focusing on the sign systems of language, he argued that children and adults use speech to communicate, to aid social contact, and to influence surrounding individuals. One of the specific ways Vygotsky presented these claims was in his account of *inner speech*. Because this speech was derived from the primary functions he described, it followed that inner speech, the mind at work, should reflect certain properties of these early precursors, such as talk that has a dialogic structure. Social, collaborative forms of behavior are transferred to the individual's psychological functioning, to consciousness and knowing.

Vygotsky's view of talking to oneself is in contrast to that of Piaget, who regarded this as nonmature behavior. According to Vygotsky (1987), *private speech* is a speech form that serves a cognitive, self-regulating function. He argued that the most significant moment in cognitive development happens when the preschool child begins to use language to direct behavior rather than just for communication. This new knowledge is then internalized. Private speech is the intermediate stage between the use of language in the world and inner speech or thought. Language has become a cultural tool that is used to continue to construct meaning.

Thinking may be observed during preschool years through the regulating language used during a challenging task. Bruner (1983) also argued that this regulatory language is used first by a knowledgeable other (that is, a metacognitive guide) and gradually is adopted by the child or by anybody learning a strategy for the first time. Private speech thus may be regarded as the means through which learners transfer the regulatory role from others to self. So, unlike Piaget (1978) who suggested that private speech becomes more social with age, Vygotsky argued that social and private speech always go together. It is not surprising that Vygotsky also argued that make-believe play is generated socially and is inherently communicative, whereas Piaget had described symbolic play, like private speech, as a solitary activity that becomes social with cognitive maturity.

A Holistic View of Psychological, Sociological, and Linguistic Forces

Ken Goodman (1993) argued that because language is both personal and social and is the medium of human thought and learning, its social context cannot be ignored. Goodman explained that it was Halliday's view of language development that had informed his own: language development occurs in the context of its use. Building on Halliday, Goodman saw a pattern between a child's personal inventions, as he or she tried to make sense of the world and to communicate with others, and the social conventions of the language being used. Borrowing from Piaget the concept of disequilibrium, Goodman saw a process of the balancing of invention and convention until the child's language comes within range of the social network. He argued that the process of invention helps explain changes in language over time as it is reinvented and modified by new users. Every social convention has been personally invented by someone, so a socially constructive process takes place. This introduced the idea of sociopsycholinguistics

A Further Move Toward Social Constructivism

Bruner (1986) argued that all knowledge, including knowledge of self, is constructed socially. Bruner borrowed the notion of internalization from Vygotsky to describe the learner's taking over the regulating role and applying it to his or her own activity. All that is learned and internalized is that which has been agreed on interpersonally. Bruner argued that the child constructs a concept of an object (such as a flower) because the adult in interaction with the child brings this object into a shared intention. After confirming that the adult had seen what he or she had seen, the child adds that bit of shared experience to his or her knowledge base. Only those things on which a child is able to secure shared agreement become part of that child's representation of the world. During the exchange, the adult puts extra effort into sharing intentions through a support system, or verbal scaffold, that helps the child master the new skill (Wood, Bruner, & Ross, 1976).

Although the notion of an approximate developmental zone has become a useful description of a state in which the child is able to do something when helped by a more experienced other, the ZPD often is regarded too simply. It is Vygotsky's view of the processive nature of development—its feedback and feedforward qualities, and its dialectic movement—that is so compelling. In contrast to the stage model views of Piaget, Vygotsky's view does not require that earlier activities end for the individual to advance to a higher stage although their nature might change because of the restructuring of learning. Vygotsky, like Piaget, believed that the process of conflict had a role in development. Human activity changes with time, and these changes have direction. Later levels of development dialectically depend on, but also negate, early levels. He viewed the solution of the most critical problem facing the person at one level of development as becoming the source of the problem to be solved at the next level of development. So, although Vygotsky used the concept of developmental stages, he had a unique sense of what a dialectic stage entails.

Vygotsky and his followers emphasized that any categories or stages of learning were culturally specific and should not be treated as universal. These concerns would play a major role in the determination of individual development. To universalize one set of categories would be to tear them from their historical and cultural context and to falsify them to some extent. In support of this view, Clay (1991) described the problematic nature of a stage model of developmental learning derived from her observations of children of middle-class, book-reading parents. Observed changes over different age groups may be equally well attributed to the kind of social context in which they live; they have been part of a broad social context that has influenced them in significant ways.

Vygotsky and his followers challenged the notion of stages of development in other ways. This notion could be attributed first to biological ideas of learning. Piaget (1978) called children's talking aloud to themselves while playing and exploring the environment *egocentric speech*. He defined this term as the preoperational stage of development of children's cognitive maturity. He interpreted this "talk for self" as reflecting the difficulty children have in taking into account the perspective of others. Piaget believed that because of increasing cognitive maturity and repeated disagreements with same-age peers, egocentric speech would be replaced by engagement in the real social exchange of ideas. He also concluded that through arguments with peers, children are confronted with evidence that others hold viewpoints different from their own. They eventually learn to adapt the randomly organized "talk for self" to accommodate a listener.

Donaldson (1978), who had studied with Piaget, later rejected certain parts of his work. She collected evidence that children were able to take another's point of view. They were able to deduct inferences when they were quite young. In fact, her studies showed that as soon as children use language to describe the world, they understand that there are some things that can be known without seeing for themselves. This ability to make inferences reveals itself quite clearly in the comments children made while listening to stories (also see Chapter 9 for comments that children made while listening to a story). Donaldson also was convinced that children first try to make sense of a situation, then use this knowledge to make sense of what has been said to them.

There have been serious challenges to the accuracy of any notion of stages of development. It has been argued that the quality of children's thinking at each stage forms a far less unified whole than Piaget assumed and that the maturity of children's cognitions might depend on their familiarity with the task and the kind of knowledge sampled. These conclusions confused the notion of age-related stages.

Synthesizing All the Knowledge About Social Constructivism

The need for synthesis has become evident through the preceding sections of this chapter. It is sensible to think that children use their knowledge of objects and events to build the shared intentions needed for social development, language, and communication. And even if knowledge presupposes shared intentions, it is necessary for children to construct their own representations of the world rather than take them from adults. A logical combination might be Piaget's contention that the learner assimilates experience into his or her own frames of reference or schemata, Vygotsky's idea of thinking as emerging from dialogues that were then part of the frame of reference, and Bruner's view of the importance of prior experience and careful scaffolding by a more knowledgeable other.

Summarizing New Understandings of How Learning and Language Develop

If we return to the earlier discussion of language as a rule-governed system in the way that transformational generative grammarians have viewed it, then it would be logical to talk of stages, because systems have entry and exit points. Development must be a movement toward a specific end, which Chomsky (1965) describes as adult language (as discussed earlier in the chapter). The difficulty is not only in describing adult language but also in describing the onset of language. When did it actually begin? In relation to literacy, this raised the question of what constitutes reading and writing. Traditionally, the onset of literacy had been described in terms of some resemblance to the adult model. From a semiotic perspective, however, literacy could be said to begin when there is evidence that a child is using print settings to signify meaning; a print setting that includes not only the print, but the context in which it occurs and its relation to the language user. Many educators became interested in the idea that children already know a great deal about reading and writing before they enter school. They studied children's responses to print in the home and school environment and concluded that children know quite a lot about writing, especially as it reflected their experiences with print (Y. Goodman & Altwerger, 1981) (see Part Two in this text for discussion of literacy in the home environment).

Harste, Woodward, and Burke (1984) challenged beliefs about stages and development. Ken Goodman (1973) had identified three cueing systems—semantic, syntactic, and graphophonic—that are used by all proficient readers, and Harste et al. hoped to identify those cueing systems of language that were most influential in the development of literacy. The responses of the 3- to 6-year-olds to the tasks in the study demonstrated clearly that the cueing systems of language operate as a single, complex sign system, and they provided insights into the way in which young children use and interpret this system.

As a result of their study, Harste et al. concluded that children have the same basic language-processing strategies open to them for signaling and interpreting meaning as do adults. Through various encounters with language, the language user builds a data pool. Because language is a social phenomenon, encounters with language mean encounters with it as it is used in a particular culture. The same processing strategies are open to all language users, but children's products look less standard than those of adults. The study also concluded that because children generally have fewer encounters with language, they have less in common with adults and have less language information to call on.

This view of language development challenged two firmly held beliefs concerning language learning. The first was that literacy development depends on the development of oral language. Since the time of de Saussure (1916/1966), it has been assumed that spoken language is a natural language and that written language is its representation. Most educators have been convinced that the mastery of oral language is an absolute prerequisite to the mastery of writing and reading. In their study, Harste et al. showed that this belief is far too simplistic and linear. The relation between oral and written language development is far more complex. Although they are interrelated closely, one is not consequent on the other. There is evidence that in a literate, print-filled society such as ours, children are responding to and making decisions about print from a very early age, certainly before age 3.

Applying Knowledge of Social Constructivism to Practice

As this chapter has demonstrated, social constructivism, as a way of coming to know one's world, is supported by a large body of literature. This overview has shown that educators should view cognition as a profoundly social phenomenon, and there is much that teachers do in preschools and schools that does not recognize this. It is easy, particularly in preschools, to see evidence of a Piagetian stance. Children are left to explore their physical and social worlds individually so that they will build knowledge and progress through universal cognitive stages.

It is crucial for social constructivism to be connected to practice. Following this approach we should see preschools and classrooms where problems of emerging relevance are posed to students. The environment should be print-filled, with alphabets and labels on everything, and also should include materials for print generation. The library corner should be prominent, and reading to children should be viewed as an important part of the day. Activities should be culturally meaningful and structured around big ideas, not prescribed, rigid curricula. They should include invitations to practice literacy. The children should work in small groups that allow for dialogue and coconstruction of meaning. These meanings will be valued and curriculum must be adapted after joint decision making by the child and teacher. This means that assessment must be ongoing to enable the identification of the breadth of individual ZPDs and the planning of ongoing activities. It is these issues that are preoccupying teachers and researchers who are interested in social constructivism today as they build on the past.

Educators around the world must make paradigm shifts. They must abandon familiar perspectives and adopt new practices that will enable learners to come to know their worlds. Piaget wrote that simply telling a child something does not mean that it will necessarily be learned. Vygotsky wrote that language is the critical link or bridge between the social and the psychological planes of human functioning. Language is the tool of the mind used by individuals to transform the external world and construct their own internal mental processes by collaborating with others in meaningful social activities. These activities should be provided within the ZPDs so that they are experiences that challenge the learners but can be accomplished with sensitive adult guidance. This scaffolding results in the learner using self-directed private speech to guide his or her actions. Children move to new levels of development as a result of learning new knowledge and skills. They do not pass through developmentally appropriate stages but can shift to a higher level of cognitive activity through sensitive instruction.

References

Beaugrande, R. de. (1980). *Text, discourse and process: Toward a multidisciplinary science of texts*. Norwood, NJ: Ablex.

Bruner, J. (1983). *Children's talk: Learning to use language*. Oxford, UK: Oxford University Press.

Bruner, J. (1986). *Actual minds: Possible worlds*. Cambridge, MA: Harvard University Press.

Chomsky, N. (1965). *Aspects of the theory of syntax*. Cambridge, MA: Massachusetts Institute of Technology Press.

Clay, M. (1991). Developmental learning puzzles me. *The Australian Journal of Reading, 14*(4), 263–276.

Descartes, R. (1978). *Descartes: His moral philosophy and psychology* (J.J. Blom, Ed. and Trans.). New York: New York University Press. (Original work published 1637)

Donaldson, M. (1978). *Childen's minds*. New York: Norton.

Eco, U. (1979). *A theory of semiotics*. Bloomington, IN: Indiana University Press.

Goodman, K.S. (Ed.). (1973). *Miscue analysis: Applications to reading instruction*. Urbana, IL: National Council of Teachers of English.

Goodman, K. (1997). *On reading*. Richmond Hill, ON: Scholastic.

Goodman, Y., & Altwerger, B. (1981). *Print awareness in preschool children: A working paper* (Occasional Paper No. 4). Tucson, AZ: Program in Language and Literacy.

Halliday, M.A.K. (1975). *Learning how to mean: Explorations in the development of language*. London: Edward Arnold.

Halliday, M.A.K. (1978). *Language as social semiotic: The social interpretation of language and meaning*. London: Edward Arnold.

Harste, J., Woodward, V.A., & Burke, C.L. (1984). *Language stories and literacy lessons*. Portsmouth, NH: Heinemann.

Heath, S.B. (1982). What no bedtime story means: Narrative skills at home and school. *Language in Society, 11*, 49–76.

Kuhn, T. (1962). *The structure of scientific revolutions*. Chicago, IL: University of Chicago Press.

Locke, J. (1974). *An essay concerning human understanding* (A.C. Fraser, Ed.). Oxford, UK: The Clarendon Press. (Original work published 1690)

Piaget, J. (1976). *The grasp of consciousness: Action and concept in the young child*. Cambridge, MA: Harvard University Press.

Piaget, J. (1978). *Behavior and evolution* (D. Nicholson-Smith, Trans.). New York: Pantheon.

Saussure, F. de. (1966). *Course in general linguistics* (W. Baskin, Trans.). New York: McGraw-Hill. (Original work published 1916)

Skinner, B.F. (1969). *Contingencies of reinforcement: A theoretical analysis*. New York: Appleton Century Crofts.

Vygotsky, L.S. (1978). *Mind in society: The development of higher psychological processes* (M. Cole, V.J. Steiner, S. Scribner, & E. Souberman, Eds. and Trans.). Cambridge, MA: Harvard University Press. (Original work published 1934)

Vygotsky, L.S. (1987). *Thinking and speech* (N. Minich, Ed. and Trans.) New York: Plenum.

Wertsch, J.V. (1991). *Voices of the mind: A sociocultural approach to mediated action.* Hemel Hempstead, UK: Harvester Wheatsheaf.

Wood, D., Bruner, J., & Ross, G. (1976). The role of tutoring in problem solving. *Journal of Child Psychology and Psychiatry, 17*(2), 89–100.

Part Two

Literacy
in the
Context of
the Family

2

Reading—It's a Natural: Reading Aloud to Children in the Home

Julie Spreadbury

"READING—IT'S A NATURAL" WAS THE EYE-CATCHING LOGO on the front of a brightly colored T-shirt at a recent reading conference. This seems to be what many teachers believe who are in early childhood language education today. Most teachers have heard of such terms as *approximation* and *immersion* that are important to Cambourne's conditions of learning (Brown & Cambourne, 1987). Approximation is a condition in which children are almost correct in speaking, such as when a 3-year-old calls his or her grandma *dranma*; in immersion children are immersed in literacy, often by being surrounded by books, newspapers, magazines, and by people whom they see reading. In many ways these conditions of learning have become the norm in that many teachers discuss or believe them without really understanding what they mean. There are teachers who say reading is a natural process and believe that by immersing a child in literacy he or she will become literate.

   If reading is a process that begins at birth, like speaking, then there is evidence to support this "natural" view. Research findings (for example, Hall, 1987, 1995; Spreadbury, 1993, 1994, 1995) show clearly that children begin to read long before they attend formal schooling. Most of us have experienced a 3- or 4-year-old child who can read at least simple texts. At first children are dependent readers, that is, depending on an adult to read the text aloud for them. Children then begin to memorize familiar texts and join in as an adult reads. This is known as *shared reading*. Gradually children link the story to the text on the page and with the aid of picture cues begin to "read" the text. In the final stage the child reads an unfamiliar text independently.

An Example of a Reading Aloud Episode in the Home

"Natural" to most early childhood educators implies that there is no teaching by adults, but parents do intervene. The following transcript explores this intervention during reading aloud episodes in the home. A mother is reading the picture book *Where's Spot?* (Hill, 1980) to her 14-month-old son. This text has a small amount of print that is in a large font and the book has flaps that open in a variety of ways. Its simple narrative makes it suitable to read to very young children.

Mother: Are you ready? (Mother has her son Scott sitting in her lap.)

Scott: (Makes vocal sound and pulls the book.)

Mother: Right Scott. Look at this. Who's there? *Where's Spot? Where's Spot?* Ready? *Naughty Spot. It's dinnertime. Where can he be?* Where's Sally's nose? Can you see Sally's nose? Look, here it is (points to the dog's nose). Turn the page over.

Scott: Yeah (turns the page roughly).

Mother: *Is he behind the door?* "Oh no," says the big growly bear.

Scott: Yeah.

Mother: Yes, turn it over. Just go slowly (Scott turns over the page.) *Is he inside the clock?* No. What does the snake say? "S-s-s." What's this? (points to the clock). "Tick tock," says the clock. There's the chair (points to the chair). Yes, turn the page over very carefully. *Is he in the piano?* Oh no. No, look there's a little bird there.

Scott: (vocal sound)

Mother: He says no too, doesn't he?

       (Scott puts down the flap.)

Mother: Yes, you put it down. No. Can you turn over the page? (Scott turns the page.) *Is he under the stairs?* "No," says the big lion. What's this? (points to the telephone) It's a telephone isn't it? Hello!

       (Scott points to the vase of flowers on the page.)

Mother: And the flowers. Aren't they pretty? Can you turn the page over for me?

Scott: Yeah (turns the page).

Mother: That's right. *Is he in the wardrobe?* Oh, who's there? (points to the monkey) Monkey. He says "no" too! Close that one up (referring to a flap). Look, nanas [bananas]. Num num (making monkey noises).

Scott: (makes a sound)

Mother: Yes, you like those [bananas] don't you? *Is he under the bed?* Did he get your finger? (Scott touches the crocodile in the picture and laughs.) No, you try. Did he get your finger, mm? *Is he in the box?* Open the box up. Look at all those little birds saying "no no." Yes, that's his nose. Oh, they have sharp beaks don't they? There's Spot. He's under the rug.

Look at Turtle. He says "Try the basket" (Scott tries to open a flap the wrong way).

No, you can't open it that way. That one doesn't open. You turn this over for me. Yes, it opens that way. There's Turtle. Yes, turn the page for me. Oh look, his mummy's found him. Open it up. There he is in his basket. *Good boy Spot. Eat up your dinner.* Oh, he's a good puppy, isn't he? He's eating up all his dinner. And there they are—Mummy and Spot rolling around together.

(Mother cuddles Scott)

Scott: (gets down from Mother's lap)

Mother: You've had enough, have you?

Although this is a short text the mother makes a total of 58 utterances during the reading. These comprise 20 questions, 30 comments, and 8 responses. In contrast, Scott makes only 3 responses, all with very limited language. He is, however, very much a partner in the reading in that he makes two unintelligible comments and nonverbally initiates two questions by pointing to the illustrations.

Significantly, out of the 30 comments by the mother, 7 are directing her son's attention to the text as in "Right, Scott. Look at this." Twenty-three comments are providing him with information about the text itself such as "'Oh no,' says the big growly bear," because under a flap there is an illustration of a bear with "Oh no" in a speech bubble. Many comments like "What's this? It's a telephone, isn't it?" are about the illustrations, while others are concerned with book-reading practices such as turning pages: "Yes, you put it down" refers to a flap on one page.

The mother asks Scott 20 questions during the short space of reading this text. Using a Hasan (1989) analysis of the different types of questions asked we can see she used six "tag" questions (confirm-verify-probe and confirm-verify-reassure); for example, in the question "He's a good puppy isn't he?" the tag "isn't he?" includes the child in the talk. There are eight confirm-enquire-ask questions such as "Aren't they pretty?" in which "aren't" comes first, and six apprise-precise-specify ones such as "Who's here?" and "What's this?"—specific questions that begin with *wh* and *how.*

Strategies for Reading Aloud at Home

What was this mother doing while reading aloud to her 14-month-old son? She was using *intervention* and *interaction*, giving *insights into literacy*, encouraging *interest in and enjoyment of literacy*, and encouraging *intimacy*. The rest of the chapter will look at each of these in more detail.

Intervention

During the reading the mother intervened in a number of different ways. First she contextualized the text by linking it to her son's previous experience when she used the word *nanas* instead of *bananas*; this was in language Scott used himself. Her many comments that provided information about the text were another important intervention. Some of these gave Scott new vocabulary about names and sounds such as "'Tick tock,' says the clock" while others encouraged him in book-handling skills. These tasks involved not only turning pages of the book correctly but also the more complicated task of lifting flaps that open differently. At this early age Scott is quite rough in both turning pages and lifting flaps, many of which had to be glued and re-glued when he lifted them the wrong way. Parents should realize that this is likely to happen with young children who are inexperienced at both the fine motor skills necessary to turn pages gently and the knowledge of the rather complex book-handling skills the book demands.

Just as the mother was providing him with information about book-handling skills, many of her questions, especially the *wh* ones, gave Scott information when he did not have enough knowledge of the language. For example, by saying "What's this? (points to telephone) It's a telephone, isn't it? Hello!" the mother helped Scott identify the picture on the page.

Interaction

The mother answered many of her own questions, for example, "Where's Sally's nose? Can you see Sally's nose? Look, here it is here," and "What does the snake say? 'S-s-s.' What's this? (pointing to the clock) 'Tick tock,' says the clock." This mother sees her child very much as a conversation partner even though he has very little language at this age. Her use of a large number of "tag" questions such as "It's a telephone, isn't it?" also attest to this as such questions involve the child in the conversation (Snow, 1979).

During the interaction the mother not only *scaffolds* the question and answer structure but also *models* the names of the animal participants and many of the sounds they make, as well as providing clear guidelines on how to turn the pages and flaps. The mother also *tracks* what the child is saying nonverbally by saying "And the flowers. Aren't they pretty?" when her son points to the flower illustration. All these strategies show that the mother values her child as a partner in the interaction even at this early age.

Insights Into Literacy

The transcript of *Where's Spot?* also reveals that Scott's mother gives him various insights into literacy during the reading of the book. Not only does she introduce him to the book conventions of flap turning and page turning but she also gives him an awareness of print and of the illustrations in the book. For example, in the following turn the mother is drawing his attention not only to the illustrations but also to the print in the speech bubble under the flap:

> Mother: *Is he in the piano*? (Scott pulls up the flap) Oh no. (Mother reads the words underneath the flap). There's a little bird there (explaining the illustration under the flap). He says no too doesn't he? (tag question throwing the conversation over to Scott).

Nonverbally, by pointing to some of the illustrations such as the telephone and the bowl of flowers, Scott already is showing his growing understanding of the links between the illustrations on a page of a book and their counterparts in his real world. Shortly after this reading Scott brought his toy rabbit to his mother when she was reading *Peter Rabbit* to his 5-year-old brother. Scott said "Peter, Mumma" showing that even at this early age he had linked the Peter Rabbit in the book to his own beloved rabbit.

His mother also introduces new vocabulary such as *telephone* and *flowers* and provides information about the various characters including Spot and his mother, the birds, crocodile, and lion. She also makes sure Scott understands the plot by her comments, questions, and responses, thus building his sense of the genre of a narrative and an awareness of the different language patterns for different genres.

During the reading she frequently models the discourse patterns of question and answer as in "Oh, he's a good puppy, isn't he? He's eating up all his dinner." Here, she also includes her own ideology about food and eating and so suggests to Scott that values are part of any reading of a text.

Interest in and Enjoyment of Literacy

Scott's interest in literacy is evidenced by his involvement in the reading. He not only looks intently at the text, but his pointing to various illustrations shows he is very much a partner with his mother in the reading. His enjoyment of literacy is shown by his laughter at the crocodile nibbling his finger and the way he is involved in the book, turning its pages and opening its flaps. The mother also contributes to his interest in and enjoyment of literacy by holding him close to her as he sits on her lap. Although this 14-month-old has very little spoken language at this stage of development, nevertheless the mother sees him as a conversation partner, evidenced by the amount of interaction with him and the kind of interaction in which she often not only asks a question but also answers it on his behalf.

The text also adds to the interest in and enjoyment of literacy that the mother and the child contribute. The "Spot" books are ideal for small children because they have large clear print with few words to a page, large illustrations with bright colors, and pages that are interesting because they turn and have flaps that open many different ways. Even at an early age Scott enjoys experimenting with opening these flaps and discovering what is under each. This enjoyment is shown in his cries of delight when he looks at the illustrations under each one.

Intimacy

To this mother and child story reading is a time of real intimacy. Scott sits on his mother's lap with her arms encircling him while they read an enjoyable book. Even at this early age Scott associates sitting on someone's lap as part of reading-aloud sessions. By age 3 he would climb on the lap of any adult who entered his house with the plea "Read bookie!" His mother even found him on their laundry-room floor sitting in the lap of a man who had come to fix their washing machine and who was reading him a story!

Berg (1977) wrote the following about the effect of intimacy on a young child's literacy development:

> When he is a little over a year old, you can see such a baby sitting on his mother's lap—or on the lap of another adult—looking at a picture book (because this is a family that expects even babies to delight in books). As he looks at the picture, he leans against her body, feels her warmth, her softness and firmness.... All this sensuousness, playfulness, physical intimacy, protectiveness, personal identification are part of what comes to this baby, with this very first book—just as the

building up of his own loved and lovable identity rested right from the beginning on linking words with physical caresses. Words are a warm body that tickles and cuddles and holds. (p. 22)

Reading Is a Natural

In the home of Scott and his mother reading is indeed a natural. Reading is very much a part of their daily lives. Reading often accomplishes an important task, as in reading a recipe or a set of instructions to build a piece of furniture, but reading is also to be enjoyed and shared. Reading also is a most important means of building intimacy among family members. Scott will come naturally to an understanding of reading by being read to and by watching the other members of his family read for different purposes. Because a child's knowledge of and interest in literacy are the best predictor of later reading attainment (Wells, 1982; Spreadbury, 1993), Scott most likely will be a good reader at school.

Parents, like the mother in this chapter, interact and intervene with their child while reading aloud in the home. As part of their everyday living they teach their child the knowledge, skills, and attitudes about literacy so necessary for learning to read. Although we know that learning to read is highly complex, for children like Scott who are read to in an interactive way from a very early age, reading is indeed "a natural."

References

Berg, L. (1977). *Reading and loving*. London: Routledge & Kegan Paul.

Brown, H., & Cambourne, B. (1987). *Read and retell*. North Ryde, Australia: Methuen.

Hall, N. (1987). *The emergence of literacy*. London: Hodder and Stoughton; United Kingdom Reading Association.

Hall, N. (1995). *Experiencing writing and play in the early years*. London: David Fulton.

Hasan, R. (1989). Semantic variation and sociolinguistics. *Australian Journal of Linguistics, 9*, 221–275.

Snow, C. (1979). The development of conversation between mothers and babies. *Journal of Child Language, 4*, 1–22.

Spreadbury, J. (1993). *Parent, child, and text factors in reading aloud in the home*. Unpublished doctoral thesis, University of Queensland, Brisbane, Australia.

Spreadbury, J. (1994). *Read me a story: Parents, teachers and children as partners in literacy learning*. Melbourne, Australia: Australian Reading Association.

Spreadbury, J. (1995). *Collaborating for successful learning—The parent factor: A review of the literature*. Canberra, Australia: Australian Government Publishers.

Wells, G. (1982). Story reading and the development of the symbolic skills. *Australian Journal of Reading, 5*, 142–152.

Children's Literature Reference

Hill, E. (1980). *Where's Spot?* Middlesex, UK: Puffin.

3

Young Children's Literacy Experiences Within the Fabric of Daily Life

Jo Weinberger

FOR THE MAJORITY OF CHILDREN IN THE WESTERN WORLD MANY encounters with literacy occur before school, often unrecorded and transient, but nevertheless powerful and cumulative in their effect. It can be enlightening to reflect on the breadth and range of the experiences with which children engage at home before they begin any program of more formal literacy learning in an educational setting. Although literacy in the home is to date an under-researched area, there are a number of studies that begin to clarify some of the complexities of how literacy is interwoven into the experiences of young children's daily life. Of course, every setting and individual is different, but taken together these studies allow us to look with a more discerning eye at what happens informally, early in a child's life, and therefore provide some indication of what educators have to build on.

What can we learn about the literacy experiences of preschool children from studies of literacy practices in the home? Most significantly, we begin to see aspects of literacy present in virtually all homes in the Western world. We see a diversity and a range of ways families interact with literacy and see the resources with which they do so (Minns 1990; Purcell-Gates, L'Allier, & Smith, 1995; Teale, 1986). This includes ethnic- and language-minority homes, where parents are able to value and support literacy development in their children (Delgado-Gaitan, 1990; Taylor & Dorsey-Gaines, 1988). We see that home literacy is often different from literacy in more formal settings (Anderson & Stokes, 1984; Heath, 1983), and we see that literacy is often embedded within daily life (Leichter, 1984; Taylor, 1983).

Many of the literacy events and practices around us are so familiar that we no longer consciously see them at all. By deliberately focusing on them we are able to look in a more informed and purposeful way, raise our level of awareness about aspects of literacy that we are examining, and understand the patterns of behavior and their meanings for the culture in which the literacy learning is situated.

A Study of the Literacy of 3-Year-Olds at Home

The aim of this chapter is to create a picture of how the home and parents contribute to and facilitate children's early literacy development within one particular context. The information comes from a larger lon- gitudinal study of children's literacy development at home and school (Weinberger, 1996). The study describes the literacy of 3-year-old chil- dren in their everyday lives at home, as observed and reported by their parents. There were 34 boys and 26 girls in the study, 34 children from working-class homes and 26 from middle-class homes. One student spoke English as a second language and the rest spoke English as a first lan- guage. The study took place in a city in the north of England.

Although the range of resources for literacy varied considerably from one family to the next, reading and writing materials were available to children in *all* the diverse families in the study. How the resources differed varied among individual families, and this variation was within the social- class groupings as well as among them.

Literacy Learning in Everyday Activities

A clear strength of the home environment is that it can offer chil- dren opportunities for uncontrived learning situations. Achieving literacy includes interacting with books and writing materials, but it also is about skills acquired in the ordinary activities of everyday life. These are not separate and special events and practices, but are indistinguishable from the rest of the fabric of daily life. They have a meaning and purpose precisely because they are an integral part of everyday experience.

In discussion with the parents (usually the mother) in this study, it became clear that when they talked about their everyday lives, they were able to give many examples of literacy learning at home. These included children selecting items while shopping by recognizing familiar labels, writing shopping lists, following a recipe, filling in bank slips, operating the washing machine, sorting laundry, writing cards to friends and relatives, writing names on drawings, writing and drawing in steam on a window, reading and writing alongside their parent, watching television together and reading items from the television, following up ideas from children's television programs, using a home computer, saying and singing nursery rhymes, listening to music, and looking at pictures and photo albums. The following are some examples of what the parents said:

> There are letters on the fridge all the time. I put letters on the fridge and he says, "what does that say?"

> He writes on windows in steam, every day when I'm cooking, that's an R...it doesn't always look like it. Then we'll show him.

> Gareth can operate the washing machine by himself. If I say, "Do an F wash," he can switch it on and do all the instructions in the right order.

Although some parents involved their children in many activities and others did not, it is worth noting that a dimension of literacy was present in each of the homes. There was a great deal of rich and diverse literacy learning occurring in most of the homes.

Environmental Print

All the families were surrounded by environmental print. It appeared on packages, clothing, television, in the street, in shops, and on buses, and no children could avoid extensive contact with this aspect of literacy. Some parents felt that the way they pointed out environmental print was embedded in the way they related to their child, doing it unconsciously like mentioning colors or counting.

In addition to this intuitive response, parents of nearly half the children said that they deliberately and specifically pointed out environmental print to their child and identified a number of situations in which they were most likely to point out this print. These situations were while shopping, while traveling, seeing advertisements and logos (both printed and on television), and when facing something potentially dangerous.

> I try to get her to read things when we go shopping—"get such and such off the shelf."

> I'd point out danger signs, "what does that say?"

Many of the children also showed their parents that they responded to or could recognize environmental print.

> If she sees Tesco, it's as though she can read it.

> If he sees signs, he'll say something related to the picture; for example, if it's of a ball, he'll say something related to a ball.

Living in a print-rich society, children are in a position to learn early lessons from the print in their environment. Parent comments show how they had taken note of their children's relationship to this print, although much that the children absorbed would be more likely to go unrecognized if it were not specifically vocalized during these early stages.

Nursery Rhymes and Storytelling

Studies have shown that familiarity with rhyme and nursery rhymes is very helpful for children's early reading development (Goswami & Bryant, 1990; Maclean, Bryant, & Bradley, 1987). All the parents in this study said they recited at least one nursery rhyme with their children when they were very young. Some parents were able to give specific examples of the way their child responded to rhyme. For example,

> He memorizes a story and can turn the pages and "read" it, especially if it rhymes.

> When I read a nursery rhyme I follow along with my finger and miss the last word off—see if she can finish it.

The majority of parents said that their children were able to distinguish words that rhymed and were able to recognize, say, or invent
rhyming words. For nearly all the children, parents observed and often encouraged a familiarity with rhyme within a home context. This probably
was never done with the intention of helping with their children's literacy, although it is likely that this was the result.

As well as saying rhymes, oral storytelling was a feature in the children's homes, with over half the parents mentioning storytelling as a normal part of family life. This is an important way in which children can
have access to narrative (Wells, 1987). It was usually parents who told
the stories, but grandparents, siblings and other caregivers also contributed. Stories often were told from when children were very young.
As one parent put it,

> As soon as she's realized what you've been saying, there's been people telling her
> stories.

Children make use of this oral tradition of storytelling to help them
make meaning from narrative texts, particularly those that build on stories
the child has already heard. Often children can then tell their own stories
and respond to the subsequent telling and retelling of tales. Storytelling
is an important feature of literacy development and is a central component
of the literacy children encounter subsequently in the more formal settings
of nursery and school. (Chapter 6 explores ways in which storytelling
can occur and be encouraged in preschool settings.)

Drawing and Writing Materials

Resources for drawing and writing were available to all the children
in this study. Parents indicated that children used the folowing materials:
pencils, crayons, pens, paints, felt tip markers, chalk, magnets, stencils,
blackboard, easel, desks, paper, coloring books, magic slates, and writing
pads. Parents made the following comments about children drawing and
writing:

> She has plenty of notebooks and old diaries. Her father works from home, with an
> office next to the playroom, and when he's working she'll get out her notebook
> and do her "work"—"writing" with lots of squiggles.

I got a slip from the bank, a paying-in slip, and she wrote lots of OOO's—filling the slip in.

Although some parents thought their children were too young to "write," materials were available if the child wanted to participate. Activities such as drawing, coloring, and scribbling all were regarded by the parents as normal everyday activities for the children.

Games, Toys, and Literacy Packages

Family homes often are full of items that can be used explicitly for literacy learning. Many parents gave details of games and other resources linked with literacy that they used with their children at home. These included games for matching, listening, and sorting; flash cards; alphabet cards; pictures with words underneath; jigsaws with words or letters; magnetic letters; post-office sets; computers; and household items decorated with the alphabet. Parents expressed the following comments:

I bought an ABC jigsaw from Mothercare to help her.

We've all sorts of games I didn't realize were prereading, like matching pairs.

I've been teaching him with alphabet cards. I took him for an eye test, and he said, "that's an O."

The list of games and toys with literacy connections demonstrates the variety commonly found in the homes and shows how literacy is intertwined with everyday child-rearing practice. Many games and toys are not purchased specifically for their literacy content, but still have some element of literacy associated with them. Children can pick up unconscious literacy lessons as they play with many of their familiar games and toys and have print pointed out to them. Parents in the study also played traditional games that had a literacy content, such as "I Spy."

In addition, it is possible for parents to buy any number of different packages aimed specifically at teaching young children to read and write in a more structured and formal way. A few of the parents mentioned that they had bought some of these ready-made resources. However, they were not widely used in this study, and often the parents who had tried them commented that their children still were too young for them. For example, one mother said the following:

> I bought some flashcards. I've shown him the cards, but I put them away—they're too hard.

The general impression from parents' comments was that it was the more naturalistic activities that fit more easily with other family activities rather than formal activities that were preferred by the children.

Some of the preschool children had many resources and some had very little, but *all* of them had access to reading and writing materials and had started using these resources well before their entry to nursery.

Television

Television was a feature in all the homes and had a bearing on the literacy environment of the children. Some parents in this study viewed television as a positive factor in literacy learning and mentioned that their child learned to recognize words on television and also looked in the paper to find out the time of favorite programs. A few television programs, whether about literacy or something more general, were mentioned by parents as being helpful to literacy development.

In some cases, parents mentioned that television took away the child's time and attention from literacy activities. For example, one child was said to be "infatuated with TV" and did not want to move away from it, and another watched a great deal of television, particularly soaps operas, and looked at books only when he was at his grandparents' house.

Although television was a distraction in some cases, it was a factor in all the children's lives at home, and in a number of cases parents made positive comments about the role of television in relation to their children's literacy learning.

Engagement With Print

Children often are avid consumers of print, able to make sense of a range of printed matter, as well as material especially designed for them. For example, the majority of the children in the study looked through mail-order catalogs and many read other "adult" items, such as magazines, newspapers, dictionaries, and Bible and prayer books.

Even at age 3, over one third of the children regularly looked at comics at home. Some of the boys regularly had the same comic bought for them and a range of other children's comics also were bought and were looked at intermittently. Much of comics' initial appeal probably lies in the familiarity of the characters and from popular culture and television.

In all, the range of printed materials to which the children had access was extensive, and reflected the amount of print that often enters the majority of homes in an advanced Western society. Even when members of the family did not actually purchase any literacy materials, mail, advertisements, newspapers, packaging, and other printed material made its way into all the homes on a regular basis.

Children's Books in the Home

Almost all the children had some access to children's books at home and the idea of having children's books around had been taken for granted in nearly all the families, although in some cases only one or two books were available for the children. About one fourth of the children borrowed books from the local library and did so frequently.

Both the quantity and choice of children's books to which the children had access at home varied widely. There were two children who owned no books at all (both had moved recently from difficult domestic situations and had not yet become established in their new homes), while one boy owned "200 books at least," and was also a member of the local library. So, only a small proportion of the children had constrained access to books, but in these cases the children's experiences with books were very limited compared with other children of the same age.

Many of the books that children owned featured characters and stories from television series and could be characterized as "ephemeral" in that their themes or protagonists were extremely popular for a time, but then their place soon would be taken by other, similar books as different characters and storylines were produced. Families also had alphabet and counting books, books about animals, books about going to the dentist and hospital, an encyclopedia, picture dictionary, and a book of Bible stories.

As one might expect for children of this age, other popular books contained traditional stories and nursery rhymes. The children also looked at and read reading-scheme books, comics, bath books (made of water-resistant material so they can be used at bath time), cloth books (books made of fabric intended for very young children), color books, annuals (yearly book editions of popular comics), lift-the-flap books, books with cassettes, and books with videos, which gives some indication of the different types of children's reading material offered in many of the homes. This also indicates that children often may encounter a wider variety of types of books at home than in a school or nursery setting.

Literacy With Family Members

When children see others at home reading and writing, they learn unconscious lessons that they can then internalize about what it is to be a reader or writer.

Parents Reading and Writing in the Home Literacy Environment

In this study reading was a well-established part of most families' daily routine, and children had regular opportunities to see their parents read for pleasure, for practical purposes, and to find information.

There was a considerable amount of printed material regularly entering the homes. Almost two thirds of the families had a newspaper available daily. As some of the parents commented, even without the resources that they might have to purchase, free papers and advertising brochures arrived regularly at all the homes. Examples of items that parents were observed reading included a wide range of magazines, books, catalogs, knitting and crochet patterns, puzzle books, professional journals and papers, and mail. Sometimes family life itself was an impetus for reading; for example, one mother said the following:

> I hated reading at school. I love it now. I read two or three magazines a week, I started when I was carrying Rob; I had nothing to do. I started to read mother and baby books. It set me off.

The parents also generated a long list of writing they did at home. This included writing shopping lists, directions, and crosswords; keeping a diary; writing notes, letters, and cards; filling in forms and coupons; and sending for mail order items.

Parents noticed that for several children, the experience of seeing one of their parents read or write seemed to have directly prompted the child to imitate their behavior. Parents made the following comments:

> She'll get a newspaper, look down the page and point with her finger and say things like "such and such is on telly at ten past ten."

> Last time he "wrote" he said, "that's for daddy" (sometimes I leave notes for my husband when he comes back from night shift).

> He gets out Autotrader—what sets him off is my husband looking through Autotrader.

Some parents did only one or two of the activities listed earlier while others did many, and many parents read and wrote extensively at home, but all families were engaged in some level of literacy activity.

Siblings in the Home Literacy Environment

Siblings were often an important part of the literacy learning environment. Nearly half the children in the study had an older brother or sister, which had several implications for literacy in the family. Some of the parents explained that they spent time with the older child and the child in the study joined in with them as a matter of course. For example,

> When we help Joanne to write, Sarah pretends to write too. We're telling Joanne the letters and Sarah is writing them down too.

Some of the parents commented that the older siblings also provided role models that the children imitated.

Because there already were children in the family there often were books and resources for literacy available across a wider age span than in the other families. Many of the older children passed out or shared books. More school-type resources were available to the children, such as reading scheme books and flashcards.

Parents reported that many older siblings stimulated interest in literacy in the children in the study, and several read aloud to them. Even at 3 years old, four of the children in the study had started to "read" to their younger siblings.

In these ways, having a sibling and being a sibling provided children with opportunities and encouragement to become involved in literacy events and practices. However, several parents explained that because they had older children in the family, they tended to spend less time on literacy with their youngest child, compared with the time they had spent with their first child. It is important to remember that the composition of the family has an effect on the literacy events and practices of the home, which in turn influences the children's literacy development.

Parents Reading to Children

For the majority of children, experience with books was an integral part of their baby and toddler years at home. Approximately one third of the children were under 1 year old when they first had the experience of being read to by their parents. About half the children were read to from the ages of 1 and 2. For a minority, being read to at home began between the ages of 2 and 3 years. This indicates how early the majority of parents in this study began reading to their children. Most of the children had storybooks and picture books read to them, and many liked to have familiar books reread on several occasions.

In addition to books, a large number of children looked through mail-order catalogs with their parents, and nearly half looked at magazines together. Just over one third of the children looked at comics with their parents. Seven children, all who had older siblings, looked at or read reading-scheme books with their parents. A number of parents mentioned looking through photograph albums with their children. Other items mentioned were Bible stories, a children's dictionary, and adult-focused material such as newspapers and automobile brochures.

The study showed that children's experience of reading material shared with them at home was varied, probably more varied than the reading materials at nursery and school. This included reading material that was available and appropriate for the whole family, as well as child-centered material. From this study we see how the real world, with authentic literacy encounters, is accessible to the preschool child.

Conclusion

There is more to reading than reading books and more to learn about literacy than what schools and other more formal settings have to offer. By carefully attending to the rich variety of diverse and distinctive preschool literacy in children's home environments, teachers will be in a better position to supplement and support these experiences within an institutional context and therefore optimize the facilitation of young children's literacy learning.

References

Anderson, A.B., & Stokes, S.J. (1984). Social and institutional influences on the development and practice of literacy. In H. Goelman, A. Oberg, & F. Smith (Eds.), *Awakening to literacy*. London: Heinemann.

Delgado-Gaitan, C. (1990). *Literacy for empowerment: The role of parents in children's education*. Lewes, UK: Falmer.

Goswami, U., & Bryant, P. (1990). *Phonological skills and learning to read*. East Sussex, UK: Erlbaum.

Heath, S.B. (1983). *Ways with words: Language, life and work in communities and classrooms*. Cambridge, UK: Cambridge University Press.

Leichter, H.J. (1984). Families as environments for literacy. In H. Goelman, A. Oberg, & F. Smith (Eds.), *Awakening to literacy*. London: Heinemann.

Maclean, M., Bryant, P., & Bradley, L. (1987). Rhymes, nursery rhymes and reading in early childhood. *Merrill-Palmer Quarterly, 33*(3) 255–281.

Minns, H. (1990). *Read it to me now*. London: Virago Education with the University of London Institute of Education.

Purcell-Gates, V., L'Allier, S., & Smith, D. (1995). Literacy at the Harts' and the Larsons': Diversity among poor, innercity families. *The Reading Teacher, 48*(7), 572–578.

Taylor, D. (1983). *Family literacy: Young children learning to read and write*. London: Heinemann.

Taylor, D., & Dorsey-Gaines, C. (1988). *Growing up literate: Learning from inner-city families*. Portsmouth, NH: Heinemann.

Teale, W.H. (1986). Home background and young children's literacy development. In W.H. Teale & E. Sulzby (Eds.), *Emergent literacy*. Norwood, NJ: Ablex.

Weinberger, J. (1996). *Literacy goes to school*. London: Paul Chapman.

Wells, G. (1987). *The meaning makers: Children learning language and using language to learn*. London: Hodder and Stoughton.

4

Growing as a Reader and Writer: Sarah's Inquiry Into Literacy

Prisca Martens

IT WAS A BEAUTIFUL FALL AFTERNOON BUT SARAH, 3 YEARS 5 months old, had disappeared into her bedroom and was busy working. After a while she appeared in the kitchen, anxious to share with me what had kept her quiet and intent for so long. She presented me with the picture and note shown in Figure 1 on page 52. As Sarah read, she pointed to her writing and then we discussed her portrait of me, complete with hair, face, ears, arms, body, legs, and belly button. I smiled, thanked and hugged her, and immediately hung her picture in a prominent place on the refrigerator door.

In her act of drawing, writing, and sharing her creation Sarah demonstrated that she considered herself to be a literate person, someone who could read and write and use literacy to organize her thoughts and meanings and communicate them to others. At one time, although my visible response may have been similar to the one described earlier, I would have smiled internally, dismissed the significance of what she had done, and thought something like, "Isn't her picture cute. She's even pretending to write by putting down letters." The statement Sarah made about herself

Figure 1
Sarah's Picture and Note

I t a h a h
I like Moh-uh-uh-my.
(I like Mommy.)

through her literate act, her beliefs about literacy, and her position in her family and social world, as well as the extensive knowledge about reading and writing revealed in her note would have gone unnoticed.

Fortunately, by the time of this literacy event, I knew more about what I was observing and what Sarah was revealing to me in her reading and writing. A year earlier, when Sarah was 2 years 6 months old, I decided to document her literacy learning (Martens, 1994, 1996). I was interested in describing, analyzing, and understanding how children learn literacy in the natural setting of their home and family. I became a kidwatcher (Y. Goodman, 1985) and observed her reading and writing, talked with her about what she was doing and why, tape recorded her reading, and collected writing samples. Sarah had easy access to books, magazines, newspapers, pencils, paper, crayons, and other materials, and she initiated many literacy events herself. I interacted with her as a mother and child do, which included asking if she wanted me to read to her or suggesting she make a birthday card or another greeting card for a friend or relative. At all times, though, I was conscious of not purposefully teaching her anything directly. I wanted to understand what and how she learned literacy through natural, everyday events.

Sarah forced me to revalue literacy and what it means to read, write, and be a literate member of society. She also opened my eyes and understanding to the powerful role of the home, family, and community in children's literacy learning. Whereas once I believed children's real learning of reading and writing did not begin until they entered school, Sarah taught me to see and value literacy learning long before children begin school.

This chapter will discuss the development of Sarah primarily from ages 2 to 5, how she learns literacy, how she grows as a reader and writer, and what supports this growth. As I studied Sarah and her literacy learning, she taught me several significant lessons that are threads woven throughout her story in the pages to follow.

Lessons Sarah Taught Me

One lesson I learned is the important role of the home and family in children's literacy learning. I began to appreciate that children begin learning literacy at birth through the countless authentic literacy events they observe and participate in daily within the context of their families and communities. As they daily see others use reading and writing to make sense of and organize their lives, children become socialized to literacy, what it is, and how and why it is used. The uniqueness of every family and community shapes the type, variety, depth, and frequency of these literacy events as well as the value placed on them. In literate societies like ours, all children have experiences with reading and writing and these experiences influence and deepen their understandings and learning of literacy (the wealth of these experiences also is demonstrated in Chapter 3).

A second lesson Sarah taught me is that children learn literacy by inventing how to read and write (K. Goodman, 1993). Their motivation to be active participants in their family and community is so strong that through their experiences with literacy they generate hypotheses and invent, or guess, how reading and writing work. They share their inventions to receive response (as Sarah did with her picture and writing), compare their inventions to other reading and writing they see, revise their inventions, and invent over and over again. Gradually, their inventions move within the boundaries of the reading and writing in their society and they communicate easily through them.

Finally, Sarah showed me how learning literacy is a continuous process of perceiving anomalies or perplexities in the world, investigating them, inventing solutions, perceiving more refined perplexities, and seeking and inventing those more specific answers. This cyclical process does not change but continues throughout our lives; we only become more experienced and thus orchestrate it more proficiently.

Sarah's Inquiry Into Literacy

The anomalies Sarah perceives and over which she puzzles shape her inquiry into how and why reading and writing function for her personally and in our society and how she can participate as a reader and writer in her family and community. She investigates her three major inquiries simultaneously. Her inquiries are not conscious questions of which she is directly aware and which she can voice but rather represent how I have observed her organize her thinking and reasoning in her reading and writing. They also represent what I see driving her learning.

As these perplexities frame Sarah's inquiry into literacy learning, they also serve as the organizing framework for this chapter. We will study Sarah's investigation into the function and purpose of written language within her family and community, watch Sarah invent how to read and write so she can participate as a reader and writer in her family and community, and observe how Sarah works toward understanding the details of our written language system so she can communicate her meanings in a comprehensible way with others as well as understand their meanings. These issues are presented in the form of Sarah's questions that serve as headings in the following section. Although the two-dimensional space of writing demands these questions be examined in a sequence, I believe they occur simultaneously throughout Sarah's, and our, literate lives.

What Are You Doing With That Written Language?

Since her birth Sarah has been immersed in a literate environment. It is almost impossible for anyone living in a literate society not to be immersed in literacy. Written language is virtually everywhere; it labels cans, identifies streets, and reports news. It titles newspapers, designates billboards, and indicates directions. However, Sarah does not just live in this environment littered with print; she also observes others transacting with texts and reacting in specific ways for a variety of functional reasons and purposes. For example, she observed her father, a professional artist, read newspapers and art magazines, write notes and lists, and sketch and paint. She saw her older brother (by 3 years) Matthew read signs and his own writing, write greeting cards and letters, and draw pictures. She watched me, a kindergarten teacher and graduate student, read books, calendars, and memos, and write lesson plans, schedules, and papers. She also saw her father and me read recipes when we cooked and write checks when we paid bills. She crawled on my lap and listened while I read books to her and Matthew. As she got older she held and turned the pages of books, helped cut out coupons, and made suggestions to add to the grocery list. Outside our home she watched congregation members sing from hymnals at church, customers read labels in the grocery store, sales clerks write receipts at a store, and waitresses or waiters write dinner orders at a restaurant.

Matthew, as Sarah's older sibling, was particularly significant to Sarah and her literacy learning. Through Matthew, Sarah knew that reading and writing were not only for adults, but that children also participated in literacy. As they played, read, created, and wrote together, Sarah and Matthew were models and resources for each other. They were catalysts stimulating and facilitating each other's learning, actively and reactively shaping literacy experiences for each other (Taylor, 1983).

Through experiences such as these in which written language is used with intent and purpose in the context of natural, everyday, socially significant literacy events at home and in the community, Sarah, like other children, learned that written language communicates meaning for specific purposes (Hall, 1985; Leichter, 1984; Taylor, 1983; Taylor & Dorsey-Gaines, 1988). She inferred "relationships between print and the actions of other participating representatives of the culture" (Harste, Woodward, & Burke, 1984, p. 143) and her "roots of literacy" (Y. Goodman, 1980) embedded in the soil of her literate environment germinated and began to grow.

Literacy always has been intrinsic to Sarah's experiences, woven into the fabric of her life as a tool for making social connections with others, expressing herself, and exploring her world alone or with others (Dyson, 1989). She knows what literacy is because she knows and experiences what it does (Halliday, 1975). As she has grown, she has continued to learn new functions for written language, such as birthday invitations, homework assignments, play scripts, eye charts, video games, dictionaries, computer manuals, and telephone directories. Although the forms and purposes for written language are endless, their function of communicating meaning remains the same.

How Can I Read and Write?

Through her experiences, Sarah has learned what literacy looks like, what it means, and how and why it is used. She also has learned it is important for her to know and be literate (Szwed, 1988), a reader and writer participating in the literacy events in her family and community just as she has participated in other events.

Sarah wasted no time in joining the "literacy club" (Smith, 1988) as a reader and writer. She did not wait to be taught to read and write; she invented how. She used the knowledge she had gleaned from her literacy experiences up to a particular point in time to hypothesize and predict how to construct meaning through written language, just as all proficient readers and writers do. Her inventions represent her theories about the literacy process and "make sense to [her] inasmuch as the world ever makes sense to anyone" (Halliday, 1980, p. 16).

Sarah Invents How to Read

Sarah's reading inventions involved children's literature and environmental print. Her love and enjoyment of literature was evident in the time she spent listening to her father and me read stories to her and in the way she became immersed in books, breathing life into the ink on the paper as all readers do (Rosenblatt, 1978). To invent how to read a story Sarah used her knowledge of story structure and written language patterns to construct a version of the story that made sense to her (Doake, 1985). In creating her "holistic rememberings" (Matlin, 1984) she integrated a semantic use of the illustrations, her experience with the text, and her knowledge of the language in books. Her "story reading" definitely sounded like a story, not like her conversations or her reading of signs and labels.

At one time I had dismissed children's reading by holistic rememberings as "pretend" reading because they were not "reading" the words. I came to understand through Sarah, though, that in her holistic rememberings she was learning to access, control, and practice the reading process (Doake, 1988) and that her readings demonstrated she was processing text and building and synthesizing meaning (Mikkelsen, 1985), not merely reciting a memorized rendition of a story. Like all readers, she integrated language cues and reading strategies to make sense of text. She predicted meaning, and as long as her predictions made sense, she continued; she corrected when they did not make sense. Her reading process contained the same elements as the reading process of proficient readers, with the exception of integrating the visual cues. Her reading made sense (semantic cueing system) and grammatically sounded like language (syntactic cueing system) but she did not integrate the print (graphophonic cueing system). As she gained experience, she wove in the print cues, not changing her reading process but orchestrating it more proficiently.

Sarah also invented how to read the environmental print in her home and community (see Chapter 7 for further discussion on environmental print). She again drew on her experiences and used her knowledge of language and print to create meaning in specific contexts (Y. Goodman, 1983). Sometimes she read print conventionally, as she did with McDonalds and STOP signs when she was 2½ years old. Other times she did not. For example, when we were at the grocery store buying decorations for her birthday cake, she, soon to be 3 years old, ran her finger under the candy letters that spelled *Happy Birthday* and read *Sarah Martens*. Although not conventional, that reading and others like it also was not random or capricious. In it Sarah demonstrated her understanding that print says something that she expects to make sense to her personally. She negotiated the symbolic meanings, the print contexts, her experience, and social contexts (Dyson, 1989) to make logical predictions of appropriate meanings in specific print contexts, based on her own knowledge, experience, and understanding, just as all readers do.

Sarah Invents How to Write

Sarah's first writing inventions at 2½ years revealed that she had learned to distinguish between writing and drawing. Observing events such as her father painting, her brother drawing and writing to create greeting cards, me writing grocery lists, as well as her own experiences with books, pencils, and paper helped her make this distinction. She perceived writing as linear and drawing as circular. So, to write she made horizontal or vertical lines (which she would read or ask someone else to read) and to draw she made continuous circular forms (which she would name or label). Her marks for drawing and writing were never random but reflected systematic decisions about how written language and artistic systems are organized (Harste et al., 1984).

Sarah built on her knowledge of both writing and drawing to enhance and deepen her understanding of the other. Whereas she initially wrote with lines and drew with circles, as she continued to read, write, and draw she learned that the same shapes (circles) and strokes (lines) could be used for different purposes, depending on the meaning she wanted to represent, as seen in her work in Figure 2 on page 60. When I found Sarah, 2 years 10 months, at the kitchen table and asked what she had written, she announced "<o>s" [the symbol < > will be used to indicate the letter designated]. She had realized that she also could write with circles and draw with lines. Noteworthy in her drawing is the abundance of <o>s with no linearity and little variety (a mark of children differentiating between drawing and writing), limited only by the boundaries of the paper (Ferreiro, 1984). To Sarah, <o> was a letter, an object like a car, incapable of representing anything else. Although the portraits are also circular, the dots and lines embedded in them unquestionably designate them as portraits very distinct from her <o>s. In using the same lines and shapes for different purposes, depending on the meaning she wanted to represent, Sarah enriched and expanded her meaning potential in each.

As Sarah continued to experience the use of literacy for meaningful purposes, she deepened her understandings of reading and writing and the complex relations in each. She began reading her <o>s, indicating that they moved from being just letters to placeholders for her meaning. For example, one day she made seven <o>s and read them as "I like to ride my bike" and five <o>s she read as "I like to play with Carl." She drastically reduced the quantity of her circles to roughly correspond to the boundaries of her message and indicated by writing with placeholders for meaning that writing is not composed of isolated letters but of symbols representing meaning, an understanding all readers and writers have. It is interesting to note that all of these <o>s as placeholders were approximately the same size with the exception of one <o> in the sentence about Carl, a neighbor child who was older and physically larger than Sarah. Sarah represented the physical characteristics of her subject in her writing, which children distinguishing between drawing and writing sometimes do (Ferreiro & Teberosky, 1982).

Sarah continued drawing and writing for her own pleasure and purposes, sometimes sharing her creations with me and other times leaving them in the corners of her bedroom for me to find when I cleaned. She began adding more details to her drawing and incorporating new symbols, resembling <a>, <t>, <h>, <w>, and <I>, into her writing. She organized her writing and art similarly to the familiar mainstream text and illustration organization in literature and in environmental print, demonstrating

Figure 2
Sarah's Drawing and Writing With <O>s (Age 2 Years, 10 Months)

her desire to participate and communicate meaning with others in her social environment (Harste et al., 1984).

Sarah Invents the Syllabic Hypothesis in Reading and Writing

At 3 years 4 months of age, Sarah invented a way to connect the
oral language she spoke with the written language she saw on paper.
While making a birthday card for Matthew's first-grade teacher she wrote
four symbols resembling a capital <I> with extra cross marks through the
vertical line. She pointed to these symbols and read "Hap-py Birth-day,"
matching one oral syllable with one written symbol. Ferreiro (1984) refers
to this guess children invent to match oral and written language as the
syllabic hypothesis. With the syllabic hypothesis Sarah invented how to
integrate her messages that made sense (semantic-pragmatic system) and
sounded like language (syntactic system) with the graphic print (graphophonic system) she saw. This represents the beginning of her understanding of phonics (Ferreiro, 1991; K. Goodman, 1993).

Sarah used the syllabic hypothesis regularly when she wrote for several weeks. An example is the note to her grandfather in Figure 3 on page
62. Her creations usually included a portrait and a sentence with three
symbols resembling <I> or <T>, as seen in the figure. She was not concerned with the lack of variation in her writing and focused instead on
connecting her oral and written language.

In a similar way Sarah applied the syllabic hypothesis to her reading,
matching an oral word or syllable with a written letter in the text. One afternoon she selected *Time for School, Little Dinosaur* (Herman, 1990) for
us to read. When we came to the page with a picture of a bus stop with a
sign reading *BUS* she said, "I know what that says [referring to the sign].
Bus [pointing to the *B*], bus [pointing to the *U*], *bus* [pointing to the *S*]." For
her, each letter represented a word or syllable; a group of letters did not represent one word. Through her continuing experience with reading and writing she refined her thinking to understand the relations among patterns of
letters, patterns of sounds, syntactic structures, and meaning.

Sarah Refines Her Writing

One day Sarah, 3 years 5 months, began incorporating more letters
into her writing inventions, moving beyond the one-to-one syllabic hy-

Figure 3
Sarah's Note to Her Grandfather (Age 3 Years, 4 Months)

I love Grandpa.

pothesis relation to elongating one sound in one word, as we saw in her writing in Figure 1 on page 52. Perhaps she was perceiving the writing in her environment in more detail and noticed it was longer than the three to five letters she usually wrote with little internal variation, or perhaps she enjoyed confidently generating more involved text and wanted to write more as she saw her family members and others do. Her writing inventions became more detailed and showed more variation in the letters. Her drawings also became more detailed and precise (as revealed by the contrast between Figure 1 and Figure 3, created three weeks apart) and she moved beyond drawing primarily portraits to other features and objects in her environment.

Although Sarah's inventions in response to her inquiry of "How can I read and write?" are not conventional, they indicate her growing understanding that there is more to reading than producing a meaningful response to a book and more to writing than making marks on paper. Her inventions also were not limited to written language. She perceived other ways we make and share meaning, such as musical jingles on television and gas prices at the gas station, and invented how to write music, using wavy lines to indicate the rising and falling flow of the melody, and how to do math homework, similar to what she saw Matthew doing. Over time, as she gained experience, Sarah gradually refined her inventions and controlled the literacy process more proficiently. Her inventing of how she can read and write continues as she grows older, and is seen in such areas as her spelling inventions and her personal logos and signatures.

How Do We Read and Write?

Sarah enjoyed and actively participated in the literacy club through her reading and writing inventions. As her experiences grew she began perceiving finer and finer details in the reading and writing she observed in her family and community. At $3^1/_2$ years she entered preschool and immediately decided she wanted to learn to write her own name, followed by *Matthew*, *Mommy*, and *Daddy*. Learning these names and discovering the alphabetic principle while writing a thank-you note for a Christmas gift were the catalysts to Sarah's understanding that in our writing system specific letter patterns represent specific sound patterns, quite unlike the writing system she had invented using one letter per word, syllable, or elongated sound to represent her meaning. She was also understanding that members of her family and community share and adhere to the rules of our writing system in order to facilitate the ease with which we communicate our meanings.

With this understanding Sarah worked on refining her inventions so she could more easily communicate her meanings as well as understand the meanings of others. This meant she needed to integrate the graphophonic system (the sound system, the graphic system, and phonics that relates them) with the semantic and syntactic systems she was already using. In reading she invented several strategies to help her connect with the print in the text. For example, she used familiar "landmarks" that she knew, such as *I, no, Mommy,* or *yes,* to help her pace her reading so her finger and voice reached the landmarks at the same time. She voluntarily reread to perfect her timing until she felt comfortable and satisfied with it.

When she did not have specific landmarks, Sarah used her knowledge, experience, and familiarity with the text to follow the print. If there was text left over when she thought she had completed the page, she would go back and reread. Sarah's awareness of visual cues slowed her reading considerably as she worked to integrate the visual information on the page with the nonvisual information in her head. Slowly and carefully she read and reread clauses and sentences, predicting meaning, using print to confirm her predictions, and correcting herself if it did not support what she expected to happen. As she continued reading she refined her reading invention, integrating the three language cue systems to predict and construct meaning more and more proficiently.

Sarah also worked to integrate the graphophonic system into her writing. She did not ask or wait to be told how to spell (a request I would not have granted anyway) but invented her own spelling system. How she perceived sound patterns in a given context determined the graphic representations she invented for these sound patterns in her writing. Her spelling inventions drew from such information as the letter name, the sound of the letter name, and where the sound is articulated in the mouth (Read, 1971). An example of Sarah's spelling system is found in her thank-you note in Figure 4, written in appreciation of basketball tickets our family received. She insisted on beginning with her name so the recipient of the note would know immediately who it was from. She placed a <Y> at the end of *Dear* because she pronounced the word with an aspiration or burst of air, similar to the aspiration in /w/ [the symbol / / will be used to indicate the sound], which sounds like the beginning of the letter name <Y>. She pronounced *gorilla* as *gowilla*, thus the <Y> representing /r/, which she pronounced /w/ in that spelling. Because /g/ and /k/ are articulated similarly, she begins *gorilla* with <k>. Sarah represents the letter pattern <th> in *thank* and *the* with <v> because she pronounced that letter

Figure 4
Sarah's Thank-You Note (Age 4 Years, 5 Months)

Dey   AsBos
Dear Ambrose
 Va   U vo v TAKe
Thank you for the tickets.
I LIK V
I like the
KYL
gorilla.
I LIK V SIN
I like the Suns.

Sarah
I love you.

pattern like /f/ in *finger*. She pronounced *Matthew*, for example, as "Mafew." Because /f/ and /v/ are both articulated at the front of the mouth by the teeth and lips, she represents the <th> pattern with <v>. Even though her own name begins with <S>, Sarah usually represented /s/ in her writing with <c>, as in her spelling of *tickets*, because of the similarity between the beginning of the letter name <c> and /s/. She consistently used <I> to represent the schwa, as in her spelling of *Suns*.

Anyone looking at Sarah's writing who did not understand her spelling system would conclude that she was simply writing arbitrary letters and did not understand phonics. However, by the time Sarah turned 5 and entered kindergarten she had invented an incredibly sophisticated writing system that she continued to refine and perfect as she gained more and more experience with literacy. She worked, and has continued to work, at refining her system because she knows that to be understood by others she has to situate her writing within boundaries that allow us to share meaning effectively and efficiently with one another. As she grows and learns new forms and genres of reading and writing she also will learn how to communicate effectively through them.

Conclusion

Sarah's literacy learning did not occur in a vacuum. She has invented and learned literacy easily and effortlessly because she is in a family and community environment rich with literacy. She daily sees and experiences literacy used for functional and authentic purposes. Literacy is woven so seamlessly into our lives that we take it for granted and are not aware of all the reading and writing we do each day. However, Sarah was and is aware. She uses these events to sort out functions and rules and to deepen her understandings of what literacy is, why we need it, and how it works in our lives. From her first reading and writing inventions, she has been accepted and respected and her reading and writing valued, no different than her father, brother, mother, or other readers and writers. Through her immersion in literacy in a family and community who value her and her literacy inventions, her literacy has grown and matured. Sarah's growth as a reader and writer will continue as she learns and experiences needs and uses for literacy. Neither her literacy inquiry nor ours ever ends.

References

Doake, D. (1985). Reading-like behavior: Its role in learning to read. In A. Jaggar & M.T. Smith-Burke (Eds.), *Observing the language learner*. Newark, DE: International Reading Association; Urbana, IL: National Council of Teachers of English.

Doake, D. (1988). *Reading begins at birth*. New York: Scholastic.

Dyson, A. (1989). *Multiple worlds of child writers: Friends learning to write*. New York: Teachers College Press.

Ferreiro, E. (1984). The underlying logic of literacy development. In H. Goelman, A. Oberg, & F. Smith (Eds.), *Awakening to literacy* (pp. 154–173). Portsmouth, NH: Heinemann.

Ferreiro, E. (1991). Literacy acquisition and the representation of language. In C. Kamii, M. Manning, & G. Manning (Eds.), *Early literacy: A constructivist foundation for whole language* (pp. 31–55). Washington, DC: National Education Association.

Ferreiro, E., & Teberosky, A. (1982). *Literacy before schooling*. Portsmouth, NH: Heinemann.

Goodman, K. (1993). *Phonics phacts*. Portsmouth, NH: Heinemann.

Goodman, Y. (1980). The roots of literacy. In M.P. Douglass (Ed.), *Forty-fourth Yearbook of the Claremont Reading Conference* (pp. 1–32). Claremont, CA: Claremont Reading Conference.

Goodman, Y. (1983). Beginning reading development: Strategies and principles. In R.P. Parker & F.A. Davis (Eds.), *Developing literacy: Young children's use of language* (pp. 68–83). Newark, DE: International Reading Association.

Goodman, Y. (1985). Kidwatching: Observing children in the classroom. In A. Jaggar & M.T. Smith-Burke (Eds.), *Observing the language learner* (pp. 9–18). Newark, DE: International Reading Association; Urbana, IL: National Council of Teachers of English.

Hall, N. (1985). When do children learn to read? *Reading, 19*(2), 57–70.

Halliday, M.A.K. (1975). *Learning how to mean: Explorations in the development of language*. Baltimore, MD: Edward Arnold.

Halliday, M.A.K. (1980). Three aspects of children's language development: Learning language, learning through language, learning about language. In Y. Goodman, M. Haussler, & D. Strickland (Eds.), *Oral and written language development research: Impact on the schools* (pp. 7–19). Urbana, IL: National Council of Teachers of English.

Harste, J., Woodward, V., & Burke, C. (1984). *Language stories and literacy lessons*. Portsmouth, NH: Heinemann.

Leichter, H. (1984). Families as environments for literacy. In H. Goelman, A. Oberg, & F. Smith (Eds.), *Awakening to literacy* (pp. 38–50). Portsmouth, NH: Heinemann.

Martens, P. (1994). *"I already know how to read!": Literacy through the eyes and mind of a child*. Unpublished doctoral dissertation, University of Arizona, Tucson.

Martens, P. (1996). *I already know how to read: A child's view of literacy*. Portsmouth, NH: Heinemann.

Matlin, M. (1984). *Transitions into literacy: A working paper* (Occasional Paper No. 10). Tucson, AZ: University of Arizona, College of Education, Program in Language and Literacy.

Mikkelsen, N. (1985). Sendak, Snow White, and the child as literacy critic. *Language Arts, 62*(4), 362–373.

Read, C. (1971). Pre-school children's knowledge of English phonology. *Harvard Educational Review, 41*(1), 1–34.

Rosenblatt, L. (1978). *The reader, the text, the poem: The transactional theory of the literary work*. Carbondale, IL: Southern Illinois University Press.

Smith, F. (1988). *Joining the literacy club*. Portsmouth, NH: Heinemann.

Szwed, J. (1988). The ethnography of literacy. In E.R. Kintgen, B.M. Kroll, & M. Rose (Eds.), *Perspectives on literacy* (pp. 303–311). Carbondale, IL: Southern Illinois University Press.

Taylor, D. (1983). Translating children's everyday uses of print into classroom practice. *Language Arts, 59*(6), 546–549.

Taylor, D., & Dorsey-Gaines, C. (1988). *Growing up literate: Learning from inner-city families*. Portsmouth, NH: Heinemann.

Children's Literature Reference

Herman, G. (1990). *Time for school, little dinosaur*. New York: Random House.

Part Three

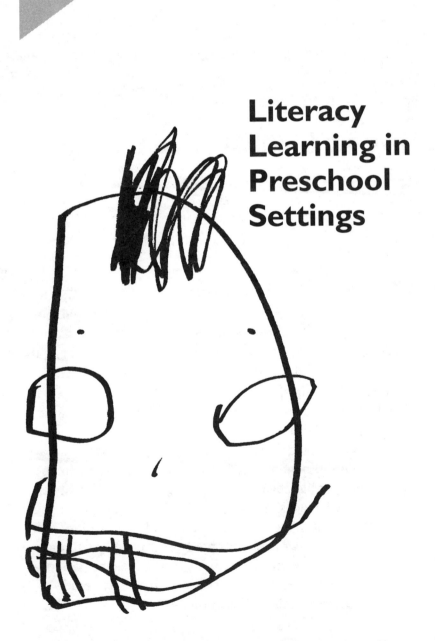

Literacy Learning in Preschool Settings

5

Looking at Literacy Learning in Preschool Settings

Robin Campbell

NURSERY CLASSROOMS AND OTHER PRESCHOOL SETTINGS TRA-
ditionally have attempted to provide for the physical, intellectual, emotional, and social development of children. Those classrooms have
emphasized the role of play with the use of a range of resources and the
encouragement of activity and experience. Using nursery rhymes, singing,
storytelling, and story reading also may have been part of daily life in the
classroom. However, as the concept of emergent literacy (for example,
Hall, 1987) with the child as an active constructor of learning (Goodman,
1990) has come to be accepted, it has become evident that literacy learning has to be a more prominent feature within the preschool (Campbell,
1996). It is the *learning* of literacy rather than the *teaching* of it that needs
to be the emphasis. So what does this mean? What literacy activities might
we expect to see on a visit to a classroom for 3- and 4-year-olds? What
roles have the teacher and other adults adopted? This chapter will look at
some of the activities and provisions that the preschool teacher will organize and will relate my comments to observations that I have made of 3-
and 4-year-old children in preschool classrooms.

Story Reading

There is substantial evidence to indicate that story reading can have a beneficial effect on children's literacy learning (see, for example, Teale, 1984). During story reading children learn about books, how to use them, left-to-right directionality, and front-to-back reading. But they learn far more, because they learn about language—new words, new syntactic forms, new meanings, and new ways of organizing discourse (Dombey, 1988). Furthermore, as Trelease (1989) has argued, story reading supports emotional, social, and psychological development.

Preschool teachers know that reading stories to groups of young children will very seldom involve only the children's listening. The children will take part in the story reading by making comments, relating the text to their own lives, and joining in with part of the text—especially where the rhyme or repetition of phrase encourages this to happen. All of this is supported by the teacher because the activity is evidence of the children's involvement and it facilitates their learning.

In one preschool class I observed the teacher reading *The Very Hungry Caterpillar* (Carle, 1969):

Teacher: *On Wednesday*
he ate through
three plums.

Josie: He'll get a bellyache.

Jamie: He ate too many foods.

Teacher: *but he was still*
hungry.

Children: *but he was still*
hungry (Read as an echo of the teacher and just behind her).

Teacher: He will get a stomachache won't he?

There is much evident from this short excerpt. Inevitably the teacher modeled the reading of a book, but the discussion shows far more than this. Josie and Jamie both commented on the text, and their comments were accepted by the teacher as she paused to listen to their views. At the end of the short page the teacher demonstrated more clearly her acknowledgment and acceptance of the students' comments as she also placed them in the language of the book. In addition, the children took part in the reading, assuming the role of "readers," as they echoed the teacher's reading "but he was still hungry."

Story readings in the preschool are often interactive, as was shown in the earlier dialogue. These interactions around the text are preceded by the discussion that the teacher is likely to encourage before the book is read. Talking about the cover, the characters, the author, and predictions about the text are all possible. Once such discussions are begun the children often will include their own agendas as they express their thoughts and raise questions. Other comments are likely at the end of the story, as the children often will relate the text to their own experiences and make comments about the characters and events.

Some preschool teachers find that the story readings are such a valuable part of the day that they start the class session with them. The readings can be of such importance to the children that the story remains as part of the central focus throughout the day. Children will act out parts of the story, use the story as a stimulus for their drawings, paintings, and modeling, and write about it in whatever way they can. The teacher will also hear echoes of the story appearing in the children's oral language as they play. Given this emphasis it is no wonder that often the teacher will repeat the story reading at the end of the day. Children like to have the familiar story repeated, perhaps so that they can gain greater ownership of it. (See Chapters 9 and 11 for further discussions of story readings.)

Shared Book Experience

The use of Big Books appears to have developed from the ideas of Holdaway (1979). He argued that although story reading was a vital part of the early-years classrooms those readings did not always allow the children to see the print in quite the same way that many children experience at home when having a story read to them in a one-to-one reading. Using Big Books with a group or class allows all the children to follow the reading and to learn from it.

In one preschool classroom the nursery teacher provided a shared book experience for her class of 26 4-year-olds. The teacher shared the book *Teddy Bear, Teddy Bear* (Edge, 1988) with the children. The book contains only a small amount of print but the teacher was able to discuss it with the children. The following excerpt shows the language the children displayed:

Teacher: Shall we have a look at this book?

Children: Yes.

Teacher: So what do you think it is about?

Danny: A baby bear.

Teacher: About a baby bear, right. How do you know it's going to be about a baby bear?

Danny: 'Cos it's little.

Jade: You can see the picture.

Teacher: That's right the picture, Jade. Is there anything else that tells us it might be about a teddy bear?

Georgia: The writing.

Teacher: Where's the writing?

Georgia: At the top of the picture.

Teacher: That's right—at the top of the picture.

Rachel: We could color that in.

Teacher: Yes, we could, couldn't we? It says *Teddy Bear, Teddy Bear* (Teacher points to each word and reads at the same time).

This discussion about the front cover enabled the teacher to encourage the children to make predictions about the text, to tell where the writing was, and to indicate that the writing helped tell about the story. She also read the words to the children and pointed carefully to each word as she read. A model of reading was clearly provided.

Of course, such shared book experiences need not be restricted to books nor used only with commercially produced materials. Teachers can use the classroom print to provide brief models of reading—indeed it can be argued, "Why have classroom print if the teacher does not read it to the children and talk about it?" The teacher also can construct and use large print sheets of nursery rhymes and songs to share with the children. Such sheets, which the children should watch being constructed, can facilitate the children's understanding of literacy. (More recently in New Zealand and Australia *shared book experience* has been referred to as *shared reading* while shared reading described in the following section might be placed under the heading of *guided reading* [Smith & Elley, 1994].)

Shared Reading

At home the story readings that are provided change over time as the child begins to play a different role, eventually leading to the child's reading parts of the book independently when he or she is older. Similar opportunities to share a book on a one-to-one basis can be provided in the preschool setting. Indeed, where there is an adequate provision of books and a number of adults to support the children, a child frequently will ask an adult to read a story with them.

Four-year-old Michael shared the book *I Wish I Could Fly* (Maris, 1986) with his teacher. At the beginning of the sharing there was a long discussion about the book. Then the teacher started to read through the book with him, as shown in the following dialogue:

Teacher: Shall I read it to you now?

Michael: Yeah.

Teacher: So what will tell us all about the story?

Michael: The writing (Pointing to the words and moving his finger under the words and across the page).

Teacher: The writing. And it says *I wish I could fly*. So who wishes he could fly?

Michael: The tortoise, but tortoises can't fly.

Teacher: No, tortoises can't fly. *Good morning, Bird. I wish I could fly like you.*

In these shared readings there will not always be as many questions from the adult, and the child will not always wait for a question before making a comment. However, Michael does use his answer of "the tortoise" to extend his comment and tell the teacher that "tortoises can't fly." Michael is also able to follow the teacher's reading of the text, and later he will be able to join in with some of the repeated phrases.

Because these shared readings are a one-to-one interaction, the teacher has an opportunity to learn about the child's progress and the child has the individual support from the teacher. This support can facilitate the child's literacy learning. A child gradually will play a more active role in relation to the print, as he or she joins with repeated phrases, utters the last word in a phrase or sentence, and moves toward providing a more substantial contribution in the readings.

Sociodramatic Play

A key feature of preschool activity is play, or sociodramatic play as Hall and Robinson (1995) call it, to emphasize the participants' taking on roles, symbolically or semirealistically. Such play is a central feature of preschool settings. The children will determine the detail of their own play, but the teacher will have an important role in facilitating this play.

First, the teacher will arrange a variety of play settings for the children in order to vary their play opportunities. Morrow and Rand (1991) and Hall and Abbott (1991) have described in some detail the variety of possibilities that can be arranged for the children, from a veterinarian's office to a supermarket, airport, or dentist's office. The list is almost endless and the teacher's knowledge of the children and the local environment will help in determining what might be most suitable.

Second, the teacher must ensure that the play area, whatever setting is arranged, has numerous possibilities for literacy. In the dentist's office there will need to be appointment cards, an appointment book, magazines in the waiting area, a telephone message pad, patient forms, dental record cards, and prescription pads. All of these will suggest to the children occasional involvement with literacy for a real purpose. At the simplest level just the addition of a telephone message pad and pencil alongside a telephone will encourage the children to write short notes. In one nursery classroom where the message pad was added to the play area the 3- and 4-year-old children soon became regular writers of notes after using the telephone. Of course, for some of the children the notes were scribbles that could not be seen easily as attempts at writing. However, after a period of time the scribbles became more like writing, with horizontal lines, pseudo letters, conventional letters, and first names all beginning to appear.

Third, it is important that the teacher supports the children's literacy in the play area. In the example I have just noted the teacher would visit the play area, make a (imaginary) telephone call, and make a few notes while talking and after the call was complete. This modeling of literacy was important as the children observed the teacher's behavior and then followed it once she had completed her call. (Chapter 13 provides more detail of how literacy is facilitated through play and of how the teacher can participate briefly in order to focus the children's literacy behavior.)

Library Corner

A library corner is a common feature of a preschool classroom. It will serve a number of purposes: as a starting point it enables the books to be stored in a readily accessible place for the children. However, this area has to be positioned carefully and organized attractively because an objective is to attract the children to the books. The covers of the books should be arranged so that they can be seen readily, and posters and toys relating to the books can be added to enhance the attractiveness. Pictures and models that the children have produced following a story reading, when added to the corner, give the children a feeling of ownership. Some Big Books that the children and the teacher have produced together add greatly to this development of ownership. The teacher also will want to make the area as comfortable as possible. So, carpets, bean bags and comfortable chairs will all be included. Morrow (1989) has described and illustrated a possible arrangement in order to create an inviting atmosphere for the children.

If the teacher is successful, the arrangement will encourage the children to visit the library corner and engage with books. Taylor (1983) described how young children learning to read at home often would take time out from their various play activities to have momentary engagements with print. Children in preschool settings will do likewise where the provision and arrangement of books is appropriate. In one class for 3-year-old children I noted four children in the library corner engaged with books. One of the children, sitting in the largest chair in the corner, was telling the story of the book to an imaginary audience and showing each picture as she proceeded—just like her teacher did daily with the class. This serves to remind us of the importance of the teacher visiting the library corner to model literacy behavior. It also is helpful when the teacher visits the library corner to sit and look at a book for a moment or sits alongside a child and begins to share a book. This often acts like a magnet and the shared reading can quickly become a reading for a small group of children. Such modeling of reading can support the children in their emergent literacy.

The library corner also can be used as a link between the school and the home. One nursery school used the library corner daily as a meeting point between the teacher and the parent, and a simple lending system was developed for parents to take a book home to share with their child. During this brief encounter the teacher also was able to talk about the nature of the shared readings and to help the parents when they sought advice about supporting their children's literacy.

Writing Center

Although this may not be a regular feature of preschool classrooms, Morrow (1989) included it in her early-years classroom floor plan and I have written about a preschool classroom that used a writing center effectively (Campbell, 1995, 1996). The use of such an area in the classroom is likely to become more widespread and commonplace because teachers recognize that it enables children to explore print whenever they wish and to have models provided of the writing process.

A writing center is very simple to establish, requiring no more than a table and a few chairs. As a starting point the center should include a selection of paper in different shapes, colors, and sizes, together with pencils, crayons, chalks, and felt pens. Some teachers have suggested that the writing center works best when the materials supplied are varied on a regular basis. Once the center is established, children will visit to write and to develop their understanding of writing.

As with most literacy provision and activities, the teacher has an important role beyond the provision of materials. The teacher and other adults in the classroom will want to join the children at the writing center from time to time to support their endeavors. By writing alongside the children they will demonstrate writing that will help some children in their development. The teacher who produces a shopping list will soon find many children producing similar lists. The teacher also will talk with the children about their writing, suggest things to write about (such as lists, notes, notices, or letters), and act as an audience for the children's writing. This encourages the children to think further about writing and to think of themselves as writers.

In one nursery classroom the 3- and 4-year-old children were observed visiting the writing center regularly and frequently. There was a wide variety of writing from the children; scribbles, linear scribbles, pseudo letters, actual letters, first names, invented spellings, and conventional words were all apparent and accepted by the teacher. Each child produced a variety of these forms of writing and used a different form daily. However, over the course of the school year there was a move toward invented spellings and conventional words and the regular inclusion of the child's first name. The writing center gave some support for this development.

Nursery Rhymes and Songs

There is a long tradition of nursery rhymes having a place in the preschool classroom, and the range of rhymes that can be used is very extensive (Opie & Opie, 1959). Preschool teachers use nursery rhymes and songs with groups of children or the whole class, which has a real social benefit as the children chant and sing in unison (Holdaway, 1979). However, the benefits are more extensive than that. The children will use the rhymes in their play as well as representing them in their drawings and paintings. Also, just as with story readings, echoes of the rhymes and songs will be heard in some of the children's oral language as they use the words and phrases in new contexts. The children also will use the rhymes to invent additional lines and create new rhymes. As Chukovsky (1963) has shown, children find rhyming words and rhymes fascinating.

A rhyme, song, or a finger play often can be used to act as a magnet to bring the children together. The teacher begins the rhyme and the children gather round to join in, so the transition in the management of the classroom is achieved with enjoyment. Rhymes and songs also can be used in much the same way as a Big Book, also offered as big sheets, as a shared book experience in which the print can be followed by the children. Of course, where children know the rhyme they can help the teacher to construct the big sheet. The teacher in one nursery class did exactly that, thereby modeling the writing for the children:

Teacher: So if I write *Humpty Dumpty*, now, what comes next?

Children: *sat on a wall*.

Teacher: I'll write *sat on a...*

Children: *wall*.

Teacher: *wall*.

Teachers will use nursery rhymes and songs for the sheer fun and enjoyment that is derived from engaging with the language. However, as Meek (1990) argued, enjoyable engagement with a popular culture handed down through the years also means that the children will be learning phonology. More importantly, perhaps, the children will be learning about onset and rime (Goswami & Bryant, 1990). This learning is exemplified in the earlier dialogue. In "Humpty Dumpty" there is a rhyme with *wall* and *fall*. These words have an onset element of *w* and *f* and a rime in *all*. As children engage with and enjoy nursery rhymes they incidentally will be acquiring an awareness of onset and rime. This phonemic awareness will support their development as readers.

Environmental and Classroom Print

Before entering a preschool at 3 or 4 years of age most children living in industrialized countries are likely to have seen environmental print. Furthermore, as they try to make sense of this print they are likely to talk with their parents or other significant adults about it. There are now a number of studies that provide details of the interactions between adult and child as they consider environmental print (for example, Laminack, 1991). These studies demonstrate how children as young as 18 months are beginning to recognize logos in the environment. This recognition when supported by frequent adult conversation enables the child to move forward to recognizing the word or words within the logo even when distinctive colors and shapes are no longer there as a prop.

Knowing that children learn from environmental print, preschool teachers are using this print in the classroom to support the children's literacy development (see Chapter 7 for a discussion of activities with environmental print). I have recorded examples of a nursery teacher working alongside children as they explored the print on cereal boxes (Campbell, 1996). In this study the teacher had followed her reading of *Goldilocks and the Three Bears* by making some porridge for the children the next day. Some of the children tried the porridge, but others were not so keen. Anticipating reluctance by some children the teacher also brought in some small cereal boxes. As the class considered the boxes the children displayed their strategies in determining what each box contained.

Teacher: Who can pick out what they had for breakfast?
Samantha: Cornflakes.
Teacher: Can you go and take the cornflakes packet?
Samantha: This one.
Teacher: How do you know it is cornflakes?
Samantha: 'Cos I do.
Teacher: Why?
Samantha: 'Cos it's got a chicken.
Teacher: Mmh, anything else?
Samantha: The writing says cornflakes.
Teacher: That's right.
Samantha: And you can see the picture.
Teacher: Yes, you can.

So, it was the chicken logo, the writing, and most simply the picture that 3-year-old Samantha suggested helped her. We cannot know for sure which feature or features she used to determine that it was cornflakes. However, we do know that she was aware that the writing would help. Other children picked out other boxes and mentioned the color of the box, the funny characters on the box, and again the writing. Subsequently, the cereal boxes were put into the play shop in the classroom, which led to further discussion among the children about the print on the boxes.

In addition to the print from the environment the teacher will want to ensure that there is a print-rich classroom. This print is provided for the children with a real purpose in mind. So, as Lally (1991) noted in one nursery classroom, the teacher worked with some children to create a notice for parents about closing the nursery gate. This notice was talked about so that the children were aware of what it said, and because there was a real involvement by the children, there was a spate of their making notices during the next few days. Notices like these also can link to the broader environment. A teacher talked with children about road safety and about safety and rules in the classroom. The class responded by producing road signs in the form of red circles with comments such as "Be kind and caring."

Part of the classroom print also can be nursery rhymes, especially when the teacher and the children construct them together. A nursery rhyme on the wall can be followed by class recitation. A sequence begins to emerge in which the teacher and children construct the classroom print together—often with the teacher producing the clear print under the instructions from the children. Then the teacher ensures that the children are aware of the print and are reminded periodically about the contents. The classroom print must not become like unnoticed wallpaper. Instead it needs to be clear, purposeful, and used by the teacher with the children so that it adds to the children's literacy learning.

Role of the Teacher

Although the introductory text in this chapter suggests that we need to think more of children learning literacy rather than think of the teacher teaching literacy directly, the subsequent analysis has indicated that there is a very dynamic and complex role for the teacher. At the very least I have indicated that the preschool teacher will

- provide an environment and materials so that the children are immersed in literacy,
- read stories and other print to the children in a variety of contexts,

- model both the reading and writing process so that the children can see how they are done,
- interact with the children during reading and writing events,
- use nursery rhymes and songs for fun and phonemic awareness, and
- talk about environmental and classroom print so that a purpose for writing is noted.

A more extensive list is given by Cambourne (1988). However, the important message is that although the direct teaching of literacy may not be part of the preschool setting, nevertheless the children are supported in the development of their literacy by the efforts and actions of the adults in the classroom.

References
Campbell, R. (1995). A writing center in a nursery classroom. *Early Years, 16*(1), 9–13.
Campbell, R. (1996). *Literacy in nursery education.* Stoke-on-Trent, UK: Trentham Books.
Cambourne, B. (1988). *The whole story: Natural learning and the acquisition of literacy in the classroom.* Auckland, NZ: Scholastic.
Chukovsky, K. (1963). *From two to five.* Berkeley, CA: University of California Press.
Dombey, H. (1988). Partners in the telling. In M. Meek & C. Mills (Eds.), *Language and literacy in the primary school.* Lewes, UK: Falmer.
Goodman, Y. (1990). (Ed.). *How children construct literacy: Piagetian perspectives.* Newark, DE: International Reading Association.
Goswami, U.C., & Bryant, P. (1990). *Phonological skills and learning to read.* Hove, UK: Erlbaum.
Hall, N. (1987). *The emergence of literacy.* Sevenoaks, UK: Hodder and Stoughton.
Hall, N., & Abbott, L. (Eds.). (1991). *Play in the primary curriculum.* London: Hodder and Stoughton.
Hall, N., & Robinson, A. (1995). *Exploring writing and play in the early years.* London: David Fulton.
Holdaway, D. (1979). *The foundations of literacy.* London: Ashton Scholastic.
Lalley, M. (1991). *The nursery teacher in action.* London: Paul Chapman.
Laminack, L. (1991). *Learning with Zachary.* Richmond Hill, ON: Scholastic.
Meek, M. (1990). What do we know about reading that helps us to teach? In R. Carter (Ed.), *Knowledge about language and the curriculum.* London: Hodder and Stoughton.

Morrow, L.M. (1989). Designing the classroom to promote literacy development. In D.S. Strickland & L.M. Morrow (Eds.), *Emerging literacy: Young children learn to read and write*. Newark, DE: International Reading Association.

Morrow, L.M., & Rand, M.K. (1991). Promoting literacy during play by designing early childhood classroom environments. *The Reading Teacher*, *44*(6), 396–402.

Opie, I., & Opie, P. (1959). *The lore and language of school children*. Oxford, UK: Oxford University Press.

Smith, J., & Elley, W. (1994). *Learning to read in New Zealand*. Katonah, NY: Richard C. Owen.

Taylor, D. (1983). *Family literacy: Young children learning to read and write*. Portsmouth, NH: Heinemann.

Teale, W. (1984). Reading to young children: Its significance for literacy development. In H. Goelman, A. Oberg, & F. Smith (Eds.), *Awakening to literacy*. London: Heinemann.

Trelease, J. (1989). *The new read-aloud handbook* (2nd rev. ed.). London: Penguin Books.

Children's Literature References

Carle, E. (1969). *The very hungry caterpillar*. New York: Philomel Books.

Edge, N. (1988). *Teddy bear, teddy bear*. Salem, OR: Resources for Creative Teaching.

Maris, R. (1986). *I wish I could fly*. London: Picture Puffins.

6

Young Children as Storytellers

Nigel Hall

IN THE WONDERFUL BOOK *MARTHA SPEAKS* (MEDDAUGH, 1992), Martha the dog eats a bowl of alphabet soup and begins to talk. At first the family members marvel at Martha's ability and encourage her by asking questions. However, as Martha starts to use her talk to act on the world and talks almost nonstop, the family becomes less enthusiastic, and eventually they yell at her to "*shut up.*"

Martha's experience is on some levels a description of what happens with children's talk. In the beginning parents are wildly enthusiastic and a child's first word often results in phone calls to relatives thousands of miles away. As children's competence grows parents continue to encourage their children to talk, for instance teaching them to talk on the telephone to grandparents. When children then become knowledgeable about talk their constant chattering can be a bit too much and parents can have the same negative reaction as Martha's family. In the story Martha is crushed after being told to be quiet and decides not to talk again (read the book to find out what eventually makes her change her mind). Fortunately most children are more resilient than Martha, and it seems that despite all the efforts of adults at home and in preschool to maintain peace and quiet, children continue to talk.

The ability to talk inevitably has powerful consequences for all kinds of learning, and literacy learning is no exception. This chapter will explore only one aspect of talk and literacy learning but it is one that links oral language and literacy very powerfully and closely. Much of young children's experience of literacy is focused around the stories in books, but it is extremely important to remember that children themselves are storytellers and that the act of storytelling is profoundly an act of authorship. There are a number of excellent books that focus on children as storytellers, but the overall focus usually is on improving the performance, repertoire, and knowledge of the child as storyteller who is beyond the preschool level (Hamilton & Weiss, 1990; Jennings, 1991).

This chapter explores young children's experience of telling their own stories and considers three ways in which such storytelling can occur and be encouraged in preschool settings. The stories young children tell are seldom the finely crafted and carefully honed tales of the performing literary storyteller, but the stories that allow children's own voices to be heard can be every bit as interesting and can occur almost naturally in a child's everyday existence. It is these stories through which children make sense of their world.

Young Children as Storytellers

Children enter a world of storying from a very early age. When a parent arrives home and asks, "What have you been doing all day?" a child is getting an invitation to tell a story. The child's response may range from a single word to a long and complicated account of his or her day, but any response represents a story. Almost as soon as children can speak they start to engage in storying. They develop different strategies to ensure that adults pay attention to these stories, strategies that most adults continue to make use of throughout their lives.

Think of the children coming into early-years classrooms in the morning. They may announce their stories to the teacher or one another in the following ways: "D'you know what...?" "You know my cousin, well..." "Have you heard about...?" "Did I ever tell you about...?" "Sorry I'm late but..." "You'll never guess but..." or just "Miss...?" In different parts of the world and within different kinds of communities children will announce and tell their stories in different ways (Heath, 1983). However, this variability in storytelling is a richness to be treasured, not something to be managed, controlled, and ultimately reduced to an officially sanctioned set of ways of using talk and storying.

The most wonderful thing about natural stories is that not only do teachers listen but they tend not to interfere. Many research studies reveal that in more formal storytelling sessions such as news time, rug time, or circle time, adult rules dominate and what should be a vehicle for allowing children's voices to be heard actually acts as a mechanism for teaching children the rules of engagement in classroom language behavior (Cazden, 1988).

Children tell a wide range of stories. One of the best pieces of research on young children's stories was carried out by Preece (1987). She was a mother who was part of a small group of parents who took turns driving their children to school. Every 3 days or so it was her job to pick up the children who then sat in the back seat of her car. The seat essentially was a private space where, while the mother was concentrating on the driving, the children played and told stories. All Preece did was leave a tape recorder running on the ledge behind the rear seat. The data collection was very simple, but the regularity and length of the drive from school, and the extensive time period over which the trips were made meant that the data was rich and extensive. She analyzed the range of types of story, which she called *narrative forms*, used by these kindergarten children. Her analysis revealed that the three young children produced 337 narratives in their journeys with her during their kindergarten year. The author wrote that "all three children were found routinely and regularly to employ a striking variety of narrative forms during their spontaneous interactions with each other" (p. 370).

Their narratives were of 14 different types. Somewhat surprisingly, given the status in children's lives usually accorded to fictional stories, only 18% of the narratives were fiction. The largest category was anecdotes. The stories came from books, films, television, personal experiences, and other people's experiences. The author also wrote that "the children showed themselves able to exploit, with skill and confidence, a rich repertoire of narrative forms and to integrate their forms into the ongoing conversation" (p. 371). Storying was clearly important to these children and they demonstrated considerable competence in telling their stories.

Another major study of storying was carried out by Fox (1993). Children were invited to tell stories and any stories told by them were accepted as valid and interesting by their parents. Fox collected stories from a small number of children whose ages ranged from 3 years 7 months to 5 years 4 months. She then subjected the 181 stories to what is probably the most sustained and deepest analysis ever made of young children's stories. She examined their structure, language, sources, delivery, meanings, and role in children's lives. Probably the major revelation of this study is the sheer complexity of the stories and the children's linguistic competence in creating and managing them. The children used their stories to explore the past, the present, and the future, and did so by drawing on their life histories, dreams, television and film, children's books, other oral stories, toys, rhymes and verses, drawings, and school.

Meek (1993) points to three important findings in the work of Fox: that storytelling has close relations to children's symbolic play, that through narrative children explore much more than stories, and that narrative fiction "offers them an opportunity to escape from the intrusive gaze of others on their actual lives, while at the same time giving them the scope to talk about what is deeply meaningful to them" (p. vii).

Given the power of stories, their centrality in children's lives, and our concerns as teachers that children gain greater control over the use of oral language, it is worth exploring how room for storying can be made in the classroom so that these storytelling voices may be both heard and encouraged. The rest of the chapter will explore three ways in which teachers can create opportunities for children to function as storytellers in an early-years environment.

Self-Recorded Stories

One technique that may be useful in a busy early-years classroom is to allow the children to tell their stories as they want and when they want into a tape recorder. There are many tape recorders that have very simple controls and are easily used by very young children. The experience of teachers who have tried this have suggested, however, that a few rules need to be followed. The major rule is that children must not listen to their story immediately after they have recorded it. They simply stop the recorder and leave it ready for the next child. All the stories can then be listened to later as a group. If this rule is not followed, the act of running things back and listening to the children's stories tends to result in other stories being obliterated accidentally by subsequent recordings. To avoid children's tears and so as not to miss any wonderful stories it makes sense to establish clear guidelines for the recording process.

Over the course of 2 days a child named David recorded seven stories. The first story is as follows:

> One day a little puppy went on to a road by itself and nobody was helping him and he runned dead fast on the road and didn't get knocked over and then he ranned away and then he saw a cat and then he ran around the block and then he went to the stranger and then somebody robbed him and then somebody put him on the train and then he got knocked over.

At first sight this may seem a relatively typical offering from a 4-year-old. It may be relatively short but it certainly is worth examining in more detail to better understand the degree of narrative competence possessed by this child. Stories often begin with information that helps a reader or listener locate the story in time and place. The beginning often introduces a central character. David's beginning starts by situating the story in a time, a timeless past in this instance, then it names the central character and describes what that character is doing at the start of the story. Already the listener knows who, what, and when.

David actually is doing a great deal more in the beginning of his story. Most powerful narratives have tensions built into them that pull the listener into the story and lead to a later demand for some kind of resolution. David tells us that this is a "little" puppy and that it is on the road "by itself." Already the mind of the listener is alert to dramatic possibilities. This tension is heightened when we are told that "nobody was helping him" and we also are offered information about the gender of the puppy. David also has slipped easily into the use of cohesive devices in which proper nouns become pronouns and the narrative is not held up by repetition of names; it has the effect of making the text more interesting and increases the pace of the story. The tension is raised again as David tells us how the puppy ran "dead fast" on the road and he then releases the tension with the information that he did not get "knocked over." We are then offered a series of short events, each of which begins with the conjunction *and*. It is possible to perceive this as typical of young children who have difficulty in structuring a story and often just run things together using *and*. However, if this series is read or listened to carefully, this listing of events actually has the effect of increasing the pace of the story. It is as if the motion of the puppy running is pushing the narrative along at speed. In the process the tension is raised again as the puppy confronts an enemy (a cat), confronts a threat (a stranger), and has a bad experience (is robbed). Finally in a somewhat truncated and unexplained ending the circularity of the composition is maintained and the puppy gets what is foreshadowed early in the story; the implicit threat actually happens and the puppy is knocked over.

This brief analysis shows that, whether consciously or unconsciously, David has, in structural terms, composed a taut, effective, and in places very powerful story. There are even more things to be said about this text. We might ask why David has chosen this theme. For several days David went back to the tape recorder and told stories; all were variations on the first story. They all had a main character, usually a young or small animal, and all had danger and a stranger. The final story collected was a bit shorter.

> Hello this me, David. One day a little rabbit ran away and he ran back to his mum 'cos a stranger was going to pick him up and said come in to my car and then he runned away.

The themes of these stories are powerful for younger children and although there is a danger of becoming too psychoanalytical about the content, young children are warned constantly about the dangers of roads, getting lost, and talking to strangers, and these warnings can have a powerful impact on young minds.

The use of the tape recorder means that there is always an opportunity and a means for any child in the class to act as a storyteller without having to worry about standing up and being a public performer. The recording can later act as the performance and the shy child can listen along with all the other children when the collected stories are heard and commented on by the other class members.

Adult-Recorded Stories

It is a magical discovery for young children that their words can be written down and read again and again. Acting as a scribe is fairly easy to do and can be done just as easily by a classroom helper as a classroom teacher. The rule is simple—record what the children say, not what you would like them to have said. I spent about 10 weeks working with a group of 3- and 4-year-olds in just this way. For 1 hour each day I sat in the writing area facing an old-fashioned typewriter. Children were able to wander into the area, tell me a story, and I would attempt to type it as they told me. The process of typing the stories was itself revealing about children's ability to control their language. At that time my typing was awful; I was slow, made a lot of errors, and I was using a manual typewriter which meant that carriage returns had to be made. It took only a couple of days for the children to understand my difficulty and they began to structure their tellings into segments that matched my typing speed and the carriage returns. They would offer me a segment, usually a completely meaningful unit, and then pause while I caught up, made the carriage return, and looked at them. My typing slowness was caused partly because of my effort to record their exact words, but it may have inadvertently influenced the structure of their stories.

Early on the children's stories were short, but as they grew comfortable with the experience the stories grew longer and became more involved. Once each child had told the story he or she was offered the chance to add a picture to the paper on which the story had been typed. Each story then was slipped into a plastic wallet and placed in a booklet. As time went by the booklet became two booklets and they were a frequent stopping point for children who wanted to revisit their own or other classmates' stories. The following section of the chapter presents examples from two children's stories gathered in this way.

Toni's Story

Toni was small, thin, and from a very poor family in which the father often was in prison. Despite what many would see as difficult home circumstances, Toni was one of the most frequent visitors to the storybook area. Toni's stories were always dramatic, lively, and interesting. Her

Figure 1
Toni's Story

My baby is called Paul

He was crying and he woke me up

He likes mummy and me

He looks like mummy

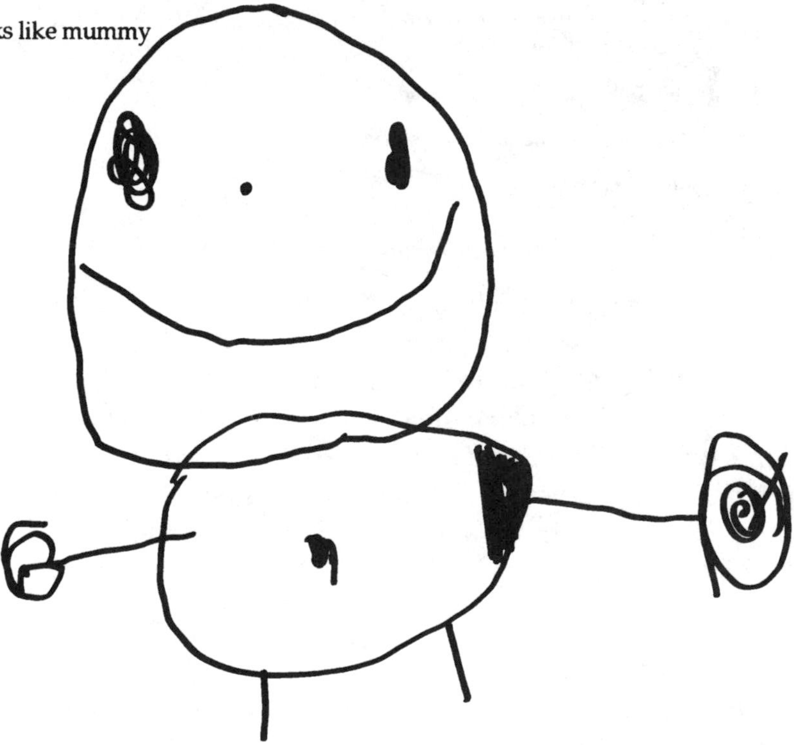

first story was simple but powerful, reflecting the importance of a new arrival in the family. It consisted of little more than four statements that were connected by the overall theme rather than connected internally through the linguistic structure (see Figure 1). Before long her stories were more vivid, more carefully controlled, and structurally more cohesive. A week later she dictated the story on the following page.

Last week my grandma got broke into

She thought someone got into her house

She locked the back door and the front door

She thought it was Burglar Bill

They whipped her telly and her fire

Now she's got another telly

She called the police on her telephone

The police haven't been to my nana's house

The police thought she had a mask on

She couldn't put the fire on

The police haven't got him yet

Toni's stories were almost all autobiographical, but as this example shows, she is not without the use of literary sources. There were not many opportunities for Toni's voice to be heard in her preschool class. It was busy and there were a huge range of educational activities set out to keep the children busy and interested. However, Toni showed that she relished the opportunity to have her voice heard; in a relatively short period of time she told a large number of stories that would not have been told in the normal course of the class day.

Katherine's Stories

The second child, Katherine, had a mother who was a teacher and a father who was a school principal. The background was more literary than Toni's, and Katherine owned a huge range of books. Her parents were always reading to her and her bedroom had a typewriter and many resources relating to writing and reading. From the start, Katherine's stories had a more literary quality. They were structured in ways reflective of traditional stories. The story in Figure 2 has a traditional character and also borrows from the magical transformations typical of many powerful fairy tales.

Katherine also could tell an autobiographical story. The second story (Figure 3 on page 94) recalls when the nursery coach caught fire. Fortunately all the children were removed safely before it completely

Figure 2
Katherine's Fairy Tale

The wizard's having his dinner
He had beer and sandwiches
And he had strawberry jam inside them them
And he changed a plate into a piece of rock
Then he changed the piece of rock into a house
He changed the house into a table
He changed the table into a chair
And he changed the chair into a bear
He changed the bear into a spot of glue
That's it

went up in flames. Katherine's narrative is powerful and reflects the dramatic quality of the experience.

The children were, like in the tape recording, able to dictate their stories relatively privately. No child needed to feel threatened by standing

Figure 3
Katherine's Autobiographical Story

I was going to Chester Zoo
We went on a coach
Petrol was dripping out on to the road
Smoke was inside the coach
We coughed
We had to get out
The fire was underneath the coach
The flames were going right over the fields
One fire engine came to help
Loads of firemen came
I went inside a lorry
I was eating my dinner with Karen
Another coach came and took us home

in front of a large group, but all had the opportunity to have their work displayed for other children. It does not matter if the stories of many of the children do not match the coherence and interest of those shown in this chapter. The important point is that all the children in the nursery class had the opportunity to tell stories, see them written down, see them valued enough to be put into a special book, and to see them referred to and reread by both the adults and the children in the class.

A most exciting development in writing children's stories has been developed over many years by Vivian Paley. She handwrites stories that the children tell her and later in the day the children form a circle and the author of a story is offered the opportunity to dramatize it. The story is acted out so the author, the audience, and the other actors make comments and raise issues. The move toward acting out the children's own words was a discovery for Paley. She always had worked with children acting out the printed word—fairly tales, storybooks, poems, and songs—but she did not use the children's stories despite writing them down. It became clear to her that recording the stories was not enough—stories needed to be shared through action.

The acting out has two effects on the children's storytelling. The first is that it keeps them on target. Paley (1981) points out that the author, in supervising the acting out, "Cannot suddenly move into a parallel dialogue that has nothing to do with the plot. He can use his own words, but he must remain within the structure of the story" (p. 167). Thus attention is focused back on the story, its development, and its meanings. As a consequence the second effect is that the stories change as time passes. This technique is incredibly powerful, because it allows children to revisit their original authoring. It represents the chance to reflect on an original composition and refine or modify the narrative; it doubly empowers the child as author.

Symbolic Play as Storytelling

Alongside all their other stories, young children are continually creating stories as part of their sociodramatic play. It is easy to forget that children create stories within sociodramatic play areas (Hall & Robinson, 1995). These can be solitary like the wonderful example in Lee's semiautobiographic story *Cider With Rosie* (1979) when the central character, a boy named Tony, is playing by himself one evening.

> Tony was playing with some cotton reels, pushing them slowly round the table. All was silent except Tony's voice softly muttering his cotton reel story. "So they came out of this big hole see, and the big chap say Fie and we said we'll kill 'em see, and the pirates was waiting up 'ere, and they had this gurt cannon and they went bang fire and the big chap fell down wheeee! and rolled back in the 'ole and I said we got 'em and I run up the 'ill and this boat see was comin' and I jumped on board woosh cruump and I said now I'm captain see and they said fie and I took me 'achet 'ack 'ack and they all fell plop in the sea wallop and I sailed the boat round 'ere and up 'ere and round 'ere and down 'ere and up 'ere and round 'ere and down 'ere...!" (p. 74)

In school it is cooperative sociodramatic play that is more likely to be seen. Cooperative storytelling is a complex phenomenon, and the fact that it often happens relatively spontaneously and seamlessly is a compliment to children's intellectual and narrative abilities. In the following example from Roskos (1990) three children create a fairly clear story, adopt their roles, and carry the narrative through in ways that make its storyness quite clear.

Spencer: I'll be right back, Dad. (He walks over to Emily.) Would you come with us? Let's go to Sea World.

Emily: Sea World! Let's watch Shamu! I'm the mom. (All three children run to one end of the room and sit down next to one another. They gaze toward the other end of the room.)

Spencer: Oh! I see Shamu.

Emily: It's starting.

A.J.:   Yeah!

Emily: There's a little fish. There's a big mom.

Spencer: There's a daddy.

Emily: Look! He fell on the ice. Look at 'em. Mommy and Daddy are fell! Oh-h-h-h-h.

Spencer: Oh-h-h-h-h-h, Baby Shamu slipped. Let's go see 'em! (The three run to the other side of the room.)

Spencer: (Patting a pretend Baby Shamu.) Oh-h-h-h! I know you're all right.
(All three children make stroking motions on a pretend Baby Shamu.)

Emily: Look! All better now.
(She pretends to lift Baby Shamu back into the water and the boys assist. They then run to the other side of the room.)

The children set the scene, introduce some main characters, get involved in action that leads to the creation of a critical event (in which the problem of Shamu seems much more important than the problem of their parents), and resolve the tension by reassuring Shamu and returning him to the water. It is a relatively short event compared with many examples of sociodramatic play, and in some respects it is more straightforward than many play events, but it shows rather unambiguously the strength of the narrative that holds the event together.

In this type of play children do all the things with a story that Fox found in her complex analysis of oral storytellings discussed earlier in the chapter. In the following excerpt she comments about the play-like quality of her stories:

> The kind of imaginative play I am describing reflects learning that has already taken place, makes visible learning in the process of being grappled with and generates new learning—new operations that, perhaps with the help of a teacher, will be mastered in the future. Not only does it reflect all this, but it can show us what children are like inside, how they make sense of their experience, and how they make things meaningful. (Fox, 1993, p. 190)

This "making sense" is inevitably complex. When children create their stories in play they often may appear simple to observers, but the themes are ones that raise fundamental issues relating to existence. Paley (1988) pointed out the following about the children in her study when they engaged in sociodramatic play:

> The children were actors on a moving stage, carrying on philosophical debates while borrowing fragments of floating dialogue. Themes from fairy tales and television cartoons combined with social commentary and private fantasy to form a tangible script that was not random or erratic. (p. 12)

As children work together they create cooperative stories, stories that have an intensity and realism unmatched by most other classroom activities. One of the most important aspects of sociodramatic play is that teachers often simply let children do it. If a teacher enters the play area it is to take part rather than to take over. Because of this, such play often has been the only space in classrooms where children have completely owned their stories and have a chance to express them in ways that are meaningful to them.

Sociodramatic play is struggling for its existence in classrooms. The pressures of time for teaching, the demands of parents and politicians that school is about work and not play, and the gradual imposition in so many countries of national or state curricula threatens the position of play. Teachers also face pressure to ensure that children learn to read and write at the highest levels. What students of literacy and play know is that sociodramatic play is a literate activity; it is authorship in action.

Conclusion

Self-recorded stories, adult-recorded stories, and symbolic play have a number of elements in common.

- They create space for children's stories to be composed, heard, and seen.
- They provide excellent experience of authorship.
- By creating the space for other children to listen and comment they focus all the children's attention on the structure and meanings of stories; they enable young children to become more critical composers and listeners.
- They lay the groundwork for later movement into the authorship of written stories and for more formal literacy development, as well as the development of children as effective readers.
- They create a role for the adult that involves respect for the children's authorship, not the recomposition of the children's words into an acceptable adult formulation.

Fox (1993) claimed about the stories of the children she studied that they "carry with them children's classificatory systems, their forms of reasoning and argument, their observations of natural and physical laws, their concepts of number, shape and so on, even their awareness of moral and metaphysical possibilities" (p. 194). Early years environments must have space and opportunity for stories to be composed and heard. Young children's stories are not peripheral to education; they are its central feature.

References

Cazden, C.B. (1988). *Classroom discourse: The language of teaching and learning.* Portsmouth, NH: Heinemann.

Fox, C. (1993). *At the very edge of the forest: The influence of literature on storytelling.* London: Cassell.

Hall, N., & Robinson, A. (1995). *Exploring writing and play in the early years.* London: David Fulton.

Hamilton, M., & Weiss, M. (1990). *Children tell stories.* Katonah, NY: Richard C. Owen.

Heath, S.B. (1983). *Ways with words: Language, life and work in communities and classrooms.* Cambridge, UK: Cambridge University Press.

Jennings, C. (1991). *Children as story-tellers.* Melbourne, Australia: Oxford University Press.

Lee, L. (1979). *Cider with Rosie.* Harmondsworth, UK: Penguin.

Meek, M. (1993). Foreword. In C. Fox, *At the very edge of the forest: The influence of literature on storytelling.* London: Cassell.

Paley, V. (1981). *Wally's stories: Conversations in the kindergarten.* Cambridge, MA: Harvard University Press.

Paley, V. (1988). *Bad guys don't have birthdays.* Chicago, IL: University of Chicago Press.

Preece, A. (1987) Conversational narratives. *Journal of Child Language, 14,* 353–373.

Roskos, K. (1990). A taxonomic review of pretend play among four- and five-year-old children. *Early Childhood Research Quarterly, 54*(4), 495–572.

Children's Literature Reference

Meddaugh, S. (1992). *Martha speaks.* Boston, MA: Houghton Mifflin.

7

Literacy Interactions Through Environmental Print

Linda Miller

> Unless adults draw attention to print and help children to associate it with their own words, ideas and experiences, youngsters may not make strong connections between print and their own lives. It is through interactions with other people that children begin to understand the various functions print can serve in their own culture. (Laminack, 1991, p. 88)

FOUR ASPECTS OF EMERGENT LITERACY ARE IMPORTANT IN MOVING children along the continuum of literacy development. These are sharing books and stories, emergent writing skills, environmental print, and phonological awareness (Goswami, 1994; Nutbrown & Hannon, 1993). Although separating early literacy development in this way may appear to create false divisions, Adams (1990) has suggested that models representing component parts may usefully show how these parts work together in contributing to holistic development. As one important aspect of emergent literacy, environmental print can play a significant part in helping children to come to know about literacy.

Environmental print is defined in Kuby, Aldridge, and Snyder (1994) as "print found in the natural environment of children" (p. 3); the authors give examples such as logos, labels, billboards, and road signs. Recognizing this print in the environment is one of the first signs of emerging literacy skills in young children (Meek,1982); it plays an important role in supporting children's developing knowledge about what literacy is and what it does.

This chapter examines the role of environmental print in early literacy development through an overview of key research. The role of the adult in relation to environmental print is explored and the implications for practice in early childhood settings are discussed. The chapter also considers the use of environmental print as a bridge to reduce the distance between home and school literacy practices.

The Role of Environmental Print in Literacy Development: Lessons From Research

Early research studies adopted an experimental approach in attempting to establish whether young children read print in the environment (Goodall, 1984; Hiebert, 1978; Masonheimer, Drum, & Ellis, 1984). The focus was on young children's responses to written stimuli in the form of familiar logos, both with and without contextual cues, in order to determine their understanding of written language. Not surprisingly, these studies concluded that the younger children made more errors in "reading" the print and that more errors were made in response to print out of context. Overall it was concluded that the children involved had acquired important knowledge about print that could be seen as a precursor to reading skills. Hall (1987) has argued that experimental studies that place young children in strange environments and present tasks outside of real life situations may not be the best way to determine what young children know (see also Donaldson, 1978). Also, the question remained as to how children moved toward conventional reading of print.

Retrospective studies of children who have learned to read at a young age have made a contribution to the question of how children learn to read conventionally. Sensitivity to books and print, arising from everyday activities in and around the home such as watching educational television shows and television commercials, or playing with magnetic letters and alphabet blocks, appears to be a key feature in a child's literacy development (Anbar, 1986; Clark, 1976).The influence of social context on young children's development also is well documented (Heath, 1982; Taylor,

1983; Teale, 1986). A striking feature of this research is the way in which literacy was experienced in the context of family and other social events, such as preparations for a family wedding. Hannon and James (1990) found in interviews with 29 parents of 3- and 4-year-olds from varied social backgrounds that many "incidental" literacy activities were mentioned such as reading shop signs and newspapers and watching television. This is not to say that income levels do not make a difference. Kumar (1993), citing Mack and Lansley (1985), has written, "Low income means parents have less money to spend on books, educational toys, extra curricular activities (such as music or sport), or outings to museums, art galleries, cinema, or theater or a concert...." (p. 145). Thus, opportunities for literacy may be reduced depending on a family's economic status.

Such studies provide a powerful argument for studying literacy practices and their effects in a natural environment on a day to day basis. There are, however, inherent difficulties in this approach because of the intrusion into family life and the fleeting nature of many literacy events (Leichter, 1984). These fleeting events around literacy are described by Harste, Woodward, & Burke (1984) as language stories from which literacy lessons can be learned.

In 1983, Denny Taylor began to document the ways in which literacy was embedded deeply in the daily lives of six families. Data collection included dialogue with the families and literacy searches of the house to collect notes, letters, and lists. The children were observed interacting with and through print. Taylor wrote, "The children in this study are surrounded by the print of their parents, as it is part of their environment" (p. 32). Interactions around signs were embedded in social events and were nearly always functional, for example pointing out a PIZZA sign and sometimes stopping to buy one.

Weinberger (1996) conducted home interviews about literacy resources and practices with over 40 parents and children from different social backgrounds. The study was concerned with children's literacy at ages 3 and 7 (see Chapter 3 by Weinberger for a discussion of her study of 3-year-olds in the home literacy environment). All the children had access to a wide range of environmental print at home; examples included comics, newspapers, cereal packets, and sports magazines. Weinberger does not separate the impact of environmental print on later literacy development from other home literacy resources and practices. However, she notes that seeing adults reading was linked to a higher book-reading level at age 7. She also concludes that "parents, acting as models for literacy, probably had an impact on the children's reading at school" (p. 151). In discussing the differences between children's home and school experiences with print Weinberger notes, "it is worth bringing their inherent differences consciously to attention so that we can see more clearly the different print worlds which children inhabit" (p. 81). Gregory and Rashid's (1992–1993) work with Bengali families in London shows how young children from a range of cultural backgrounds have opportunities to notice print in the home language in and around the home and in the local community.

The different literacy practices experienced by 4-year-old Gurdeep are reported by Minns (1997) in a study of the literacy lives of five young children. She describes these practices as being embedded in the set of institutions and relations that form a child's family and culture. They arise from the religious, domestic, leisure, and work life of his or her family. For example, Gurdeep is surrounded by English and Punjabi newspapers and writing on household items. He sees his parents writing in Punjabi and tries to copy it. When he goes to the temple he sees notices in Punjabi and English saying "Silence please." Minns notes that such notices not only transmit a language message but also a cultural message about traditions and appropriate behavior. She goes on to say this will aid Gurdeep's understanding of public print when he sees notices in other contexts, such as school.

Studies involving parents as researchers reduce the intrusion into family lives (Bissex, 1980; Lass, 1983; Payton, 1984). However, generalizations of these research findings to other children and their family literacy practices are exchanged for rich portraits of individual children and their families (Bassey, 1981). Laminack (1991) recorded his son Zachary's responses to the many different forms of print that he encountered from the age of 15 months. Collected observations of my younger daughter Katie from the age of 3 to 5 years illustrate her everyday engagements with both the function and form of print (Miller, 1996). Examples include the following:

- referring to carrier bags as "bags with writing";
- "reading" the instructions on a card game;

- suspending letter-shaped spaghetti on her fork and noting that "This is writing";
- checking the newspaper to see when her favorite program is on television; and
- filling in endless forms that are included in junk mail.

This brief overview of research indicates the following:

- the need for an environment that enables the child to experience the functional meaning of print in everyday life;
- the need for the provision of opportunities to interact with print; and
- the importance of a sensitive, supportive, and responsive adult.

Children as Active Literacy Learners

There is no doubt that young children are active literacy learners and risk takers, testing hypotheses about print in the environment and making good guesses about what they might mean (Harste et al., 1984; Vygotsky, 1934/1978). Roberts (1995) argues that in order to learn effectively children need to take manageable risks supported by adults. Returning from vacation on an airplane Katie, at age $3^{1}/_{2}$ noticed safety instructions on the back of the seats and said, "Does that say mummy's seat, daddy's seat, girl's seat, lady's seat, man's seat?" (Miller, 1996). Laminack (1991) offers a similar anecdote in which his son rubbed his hand across the word *Escort* on a family friend's car and said, "Hey Daddy, that says Theresa's car" (p. 18). As Laminack observed, such errors are like microscopes that allow us to see how children are constructing meaning from what they know from past encounters with print. Katie used previous knowledge and experience with labels to make sense of the notices in the airplane. It was a reasonable hypothesis that they might be telling people where to sit. Praising her for her good attempts and offering supportive feedback will encourage further risk taking. Roberts (1995) has written that important moments of achievement need recognition; therefore, adults need to watch, listen, and respond to children in ways that take them forward in their literacy learning.

Many educators agree that one important function of environmental print is that it enables the child to behave like a reader, allowing parents and others to praise the child's efforts. This may help to build a positive, risk-taking attitude toward reading. In other words, an important function of environmental print in the preschool years could be the use to which it is put by significant adults.

Environmental Print Diaries

In the spring of 1995 the parents of the nursery school students in the university in which I work were invited to keep environmental print diaries for a period of two school terms (see Figure 1 on page 106). Thirteen parents attended a preliminary workshop and all expressed an interest in keeping a diary. Through inviting shared anecdotes environmental print was defined. For example, one parent told how, when shopping for a dress for herself with her 3-year-old daughter, the child noticed the size 12 label in the dress and asked, "Does that say age 27?" The child was drawing from her own experience of shopping for age-sized clothing.

Cathy Nutbrown of the University of Sheffield's Raising Early Achievement in Literacy (REAL) project has found that parents may have difficulty in keeping diaries (personal communication, 1996). However, Phillips and McNaughton (1990) were successful in encouraging 10 parents to maintain a diary relating to storybook reading for 28 days, and book-sharing notebooks were kept by 9 parents of preschool children over a 9-month period (Miller, 1992). In my study a total of 9 diaries were kept for 4 girls and 5 boys, from 6 families. The children's ages ranged from 2½ to 4½ years (Brooke, a 2½-year-old sister was included). Entries ranged in number from 1 to 8 and all but 2 diaries included print samples. Some entries included examples of environmental print created by the children, for example a notice for a rabbit hut (see Figure 2 on page 107).

This small-scale study attempted to obtain more detailed information about how children move from gross approximations with print to conventional reading. A small self-selected group of white, largely middle class parents participated. In the diaries parents were asked to note what the parent did or said, what the child noticed, and where the incident took place. They were asked to write their comments on one side of the page

Figure 1
An Environmental Print Diary

Figure 2
A Notice for a Rabbit Hut

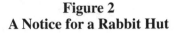

10.6.95. Jake.
This was attached to our rabbit
cage and apparently says
"This is a dangerous rabbit who
digs burrows"
He then said he had written a
munching mike a jumping Jim
and some yellow yo-yo men.
(He usually only uses the
letters of his own name
so this was something new)

under the headings provided (see Figure 3 on page 108). The parents also were asked to stick the relevant sample of print where possible on the reverse side of the comment page. For Brooke's diary shown in Figure 3, this was a stick-on paper badge with an elephant saying, "I've been good at the doctor's today" (see Figure 4 on page 109).

Figure 3
A Parent's Written Comments

- What did s/he notice?   date: 7/5/95

    She noticed the badges given
    out at the bloods clinic.
    She said   " It says Elephant "

- What did you do / say?

    " Well done — yes it is an Elephant
    but it actually says — 'I've been
    good at the doctor's today'."

- Where did it happen?

    At the blood clinic, Watford General.

Figure 4
Stick-On Badge From Brooke's Diary

What Did the Child Notice?

All interactions in the study were initiated by the children, either by commenting on the print or object related to it or by asking "What does that say?" Most incidents related to print on packaging such as food, household objects, and signs. A smaller number of incidents centered around clothing labels. It is difficult to determine from the diary records how much the children were "reading" the logos rather than the print. It sometimes appeared that the children were relying on the whole context of the sign or packaging, for example in "reading" the print embedded in the familiar logo of a supermarket carrying bag. Matching or word-recognition skills were featured, as when 4-year-old Benjamin, while watching a television commercial for a washing powder said his family had a packet in the kitchen cupboard. Four-year-old Hannah's family was watching a European football match when Hannah noticed the advertisements around the edge of the field; she read *McDonalds* and *Coca-Cola* without hesitation. This family's response was enthusiastic; they wrote, "We all cheered and said she was ready for school!"

There was evidence of letter discrimination skills. Brooke, age 2, responded excitedly to a car license plate by saying "Cars—they have a W's letters." In another example, 4-year-old Michael picked out "*M* for *Michael*" both on food packets and outdoor signs. On one occasion he followed a letter recognition by writing a page of letter *M*s. Two months later he saw an *H* on a hospital sign and said, "Look, there's a Hairy Hat man," referring to a popular phonics teaching scheme that features storybooks centered around letter characters. Later, he also asked, "Can I have an apple with B?" having noticed the sticker on the apple began with this letter.

Some children had a general notion about what print is and does and were developing concepts about letters, words, and reading; "What does that say?" was a recurring question. Goodman (1984) noted that "say" is used by young children to refer to "read" when talking about written language. Four-year-old Pip asked for a tray "with letters on it" like the one in a shop window and said to his mother, "you read it." He later pointed out "red letters" on a road sign. Two-year-old Brooke noticed the letters on her new paint box and said "letters and colors and stories." Four-year-old Jake, when eating his favorite snack in the car said, "It says *Quavers* there doesn't it? I can read the green letters now because I am a big boy now." He also said about a lottery ticket, "Jackpot is a funny word."

Labels and signs elicited some interesting responses as the following examples illustrate. There was a very reasonable expectation that the labels would contain information relating to the object on which they were placed, for example, "Brooke's pants." It was clear that most of the children had learned that print conveys meaning. Jake asked of the *No Smoking* sign, "What does that say" and then asked if there was a *No Burping* sign "'cos I just burped."

Where Did It Happen?

The diaries support the view that literacy interactions around environmental print are taking place in a wide range of everyday contexts such as walking along a road, traveling in and parking a car, getting dressed, preparing and eating food, shopping, and playing with toys.

What Did the Parents Do and Say?

The parents' responses to what the children noticed would seem to be the most crucial feature of the diaries. These are best illustrated through the following language stories of selected students from which literacy lessons can be derived (Harste et al., 1984).

Jake   After Jake's comments while eating his favorite snack, as mentioned earlier, his mother affirmed his response and offered contingent reinforcement by saying "Well done Jake, that's right."

Brooke   Two and a half-year-old Brooke noticed the badges given out at the blood donor clinic and said "It says elephant." Here Brooke has made a reasonable hypothesis about what the badge says on the basis of the picture of an elephant (see Figures 3 and 4).

Contingent reinforcement also is offered by Brooke's mother as she says "Well done—yes, it is an elephant." However, she then adds "but it actually says, 'I've been good at the doctor's today.'" This is evidence of what Tamburrini calls an "extending style," in which the adult uses the child's theme to elaborate and extend the child's ideas and interest (Roberts & Tamburrini, 1981, cited in Bruce, 1987). Also, Brooke's mother offers direct information as she tells her what the words say. This pattern of responding is repeated in other incidents with Brooke and her mother, for example, positive reinforcement and extension through direct information. In another incident in her bedroom Brooke noticed the label on her pants and said "It says Brooke's pants" to which her mother replied, "Very good, but it really says Mothercare—ages 18–24 months." Gura (1996) suggests that some responses, such as informational feedback, are more likely to encourage learning than others.

Leonie   Leonie, age 4, noticed the *Adams* apple logo on a T-shirt and said "I know this was bought from the shop in the Harlequin center."

Leonie's mother questions her about how she had determined where the T-shirt came from. Leonie pointed to the apple logo. Here Leonie's mother is exploring Leonie's strategies for figuring out the meaning of the label (Gura, 1996). She comments that Leonie is relying on the logo to "read" the label. This could have been a good opportunity to extend her learning and point out the word *Adams*.

Lewis   Three-year-old Lewis's diary was of particular interest in that, although the same sort of opportunities arose as in the other diaries, there was no focus on the print either by Lewis or his mother. Interest centered around pictures on the food packets and their contents. He was identified by the nursery as needing particular support in his literacy development.

What Can Be Learned?

This small-scale study falls into Bassey's (1981) category of "descriptive" research. It allows only a glimpse into interactions around environmental print with a small group of parents and children. It is possible that these interactions may bear some relation to those in other families, but this cannot be assumed (Bassey, 1981). Nevertheless, some conclusions from the study are discussed in the following pages.

Supporting Parents

Ball (1994) has written that parents need to be "warm demanders" (p. 42) who will optimize the unreturnable, teachable moment. The diaries suggest that some parents slip easily into this role, supporting and extending literacy development through literacy lessons that are finely tuned to their children's interests. If these interactions are typical and are multiplied into many other similar incidents with print, their significance has both positive and negative implications for the transmission of literacy through family practices (Weinberger, 1996). For example, Brooke's mother repeatedly uses extending strategies and direct instruction in her responses. In contrast, Lewis's diary suggests many missed opportunities for interacting with print.

The wealth of information about print that many young children acquire from being with parents and caregivers in the preschool years is gaining formal recognition through projects involving parents in aspects of literacy development. These have been reported in some detail in Miller (1996). Weinberger's (1996) study offers evidence in some families for the intergenerational transmission of literacy difficulties, despite parents' best efforts. Lewis's diary offers some support for this. This suggests a need to harness parents' concerns and efforts through forms of support that take account of family context and culture. The Sheffield Early Literacy Development Project (Weinberger, Hannon, & Nutbrown, 1990) focused on working with parents and their preschool children in three key aspects of emerging literacy—writing, sharing books, and environmental print—

through home visits and group meetings. Activities around environmental print included, for example, cutting out pictures and captions from magazines and newspapers and putting them into scrapbooks, encouraging parents to point out signs when traveling on the bus, and looking at labels. As one parent said, "We read all sorts now from the top of the bus. We look for words" (Weinberger et al., 1990, p. 11).

An important feature of environmental print is that it is contextualized print that can be personally meaningful for children. For example, looking for a specific cereal brand in the supermarket gets children what they want for breakfast in the coming week. The potential of this type of situation is recognized by some family literacy initiatives such as the Shopping to Read Programme launched in England by Birmingham Community Education with sponsorship from a major supermarket. It is based on the notion that although asking a parent to help their child to read may cause anxiety, shopping for groceries may be viewed as a more pleasurable experience. Project materials include games and worksheets based on the shopping trip; for example, playing games such as "I Spy" or identifying labels on packages of familiar items (Strongin Dodds, 1994).

The Adult Literacy Basic Skills Unit is funding a number of projects involving parents and children learning together about literacy. The Read and Write Together Pack (Buckton, n.d.) is an activity pack focusing on aspects of early literacy development; for example, activities encourage parents to look for familiar signs and symbols such as *Bus Stop* and *Exit* in the local area. Skills sheets are included that invite parents to note what their children already know about literacy; for example, parents may color in the relevant section on the sheet to show that their child notices some letters on signs and labels. In this way parents can keep a record of their child's literacy development. Such initiatives can empower parents and help them to take an active part in helping their children's development and literacy learning.

Implications for Practice in Preschool Settings

The environmental print diaries indicated that for some children the home and surrounding environment can offer rich and natural settings for learning about print in supportive contexts. The preschool or early-years setting also generates its own environmental print. Labeling displays and storage facilities provide opportunities to observe if the children are linking the print with the relevant objects. For example, encouraging children to put bricks back into a labeled container supports them in seeing the form of the word *bricks* and to understand its function in that context. Changing the birthday chart, finding the correct day of the week, or recording how many children are in the class or group that day allows the adult to observe the children reading and using print. If children are provided with opportunities to play and interact within print-rich environments adults then can record what they know and plan for future development (Hall, 1991). Exposure to print-rich play settings has been shown to enhance children's knowledge of environmental print and to increase literacy interactions with print (Hall, 1991; Vukelich, 1994). These settings can include posters, packets, notices, newspapers in a variety of languages, and other examples of environmental print that often can be obtained freely. It is worth noting that Vukelich (1994) found that some settings, such as a post office, seem to particularly enhance children's ability to read print, possibly because more literacy opportunities arise.

Environmental print in preschool groups can provide a bridge between home and school and can reduce the difference between the two different print worlds (Weinberger, 1996). Environmental print can tap into children's previous experiences on entry to the unfamiliar world of preschool. Kirkland, Aldridge, and Kuby (1991) and Kuby, Aldridge, and Snyder (1994) offer a number of practical proposals for incorporating environmental print from home into the preschool group setting. These include displaying familiar logos on bulletin boards and encouraging children to bring in their own logos for display and discussion. Carrying out a "print audit" of the room may be helpful in looking for enrichment opportunities (Miller, 1996). For example, ask questions such as the following:

How much print is there in the room?

Does it vary in type?

Is it at the children's eye level?

Can use be made of hanging labels, perhaps with objects attached (for example, a paint brush to denote the painting area)?

Are boxes, drawers, and storage containers labeled? (Pictures, photographs, or objects to indicate contents can provide further support.)

Are there scenarios to support literacy play? (for example a cafe, hairdresser, or flower shop). Do they contain related environmental print such as menus, posters, seed packets, or newspapers that reflect the culture and home language of the children?

The Adults' Role in Preschool Group Settings

It would be a misconception to assume that provision for literacy is sufficient for literacy to emerge. I (Miller, 1996) have described the role of the adult in providing for, modeling, and supporting literacy development through strategies such as encouragement and direct instruction. Neuman and Roskos (1993) note how the "reading" of environmental print is heavily reliant on context cues involving place, participants, and purpose. Also, as was seen from the environmental print diaries discussed earlier, not all families are able to offer equal opportunities for interacting with print. In order to further reduce the distance between the two different print worlds of home and school, Neuman and Roskos used parents as teachers within a Head Start project. It was found that the parents' active engagement in "office" settings influenced the children's ability to read environmental print and to label functional items. Parents' natural teaching styles were capitalized on, including the use of direct instruction, thus reflecting the children's cultural and social context. Using Vygotsky's model of the Zone of Proximal Development, the authors argue for children engaging in their own meaning making alongside a more didactic adult-led approach that helps children to make the transition to word learning (see Chapter 1 for further discussion on the Zone of Proximal Development). Thus the "zone" could be used to identify behaviors in need of instruction. An interesting parallel can be seen here with the interactions in Brooke's diary. While accepting and rewarding Brooke's good guess about the meaning of the writing on the elephant badge, her mother uses direct instruction to tell her what the writing actually says.

The use of a "more knowledgeable other" in a kindergarten setting was found by Vukelich (1994) to influence the children's ability to read environmental print both in and out of context. Kuby et al.'s (1994) findings also support this view, as they found that training teachers to use environmental print in the curriculum enhanced children's recognition of print out of context. In the preface to her book *Family Literacy*, Taylor (1983) writes, "From T-shirts to bubble gum wrappers, children live in a world fashioned in print. Few can escape the abundance of words that fill their homes, and yet we know very little about that world and its effects on learning to read and write in school." More recent studies suggest the role of the adult as the crucial link between home and school, in both providing for and supporting opportunities to help children make meaning from the print they see around them.

Summary

Print in the environment is a readily accessible and valuable resource for learning about what written language does in everyday contexts. The environmental print diaries described in this chapter support the view that exposure to opportunities with print will not be equal for all children. Group settings therefore will need to take into account children's previous and current home experiences with print, including acknowledging and building on parents' interactional styles. Settings then can be created that are compatible with those of the family and home community (Neuman & Roskos, 1993) and that empower all parents to engage in the process of helping their children to become literate.

References

Adams, M.J. (1990). *Beginning to read*. London: Heinemann.

Anbar, A. (1986). Reading acquisition of pre-school children without systematic instruction. *Early Childhood Research Quarterly, 1*, 69–83.

Ball, C. (1994). *Start right: The importance of early learning*. London: The Royal Society for the Encouragement of Arts, Manufactures, and Commerce..

Bassey, M. (1981). Pedagogic research: On the relative merits of search for generalisation and study of single events. *Oxford Review of Education, 7*(1), 73–93.

Bissex, G.L. (1980). *GNYS AT WRK: A child learns to read and write*. Cambridge, MA: Harvard University Press.

Bruce, T. (1987). *Early childhood education*. London: Hodder and Stoughton.

Buckton, C. (no date). *Read and write together.* London: The Basic Skills Unit.

Clark, M.M. (1976). *Young fluent readers.* London: Heinemann.

Donaldson, M. (1978). *Children's minds.* Glasgow, Scotland: Fontana/Collins.

Goodall, M. (1984). Can four year olds "read" words in the environment? *The Reading Teacher, 37,* 478–482.

Goodman, Y. (1984). The development of initial literacy. In H. Goelman, A. Oberg, & F. Smith (Eds.), *Awakening to literacy* (pp. 102–110). London: Heinemann.

Goswami, U. (1994). Phonological skills, analogies and reading development. *Reading, 28*(2), 32–37.

Gregory, E., & Rashid, N. (1992–1993) The Tower Hamlets work: Monolingual schooling, multilingual homes. In E. Gregory, J. Lathwell, J. Mace, & N. Rashid (Eds.), *Literacy at home and at school.* London: University of London, Goldsmiths College Faculty of Education.

Gura, P. (1996). What I want for Cinderella: Self esteem and self assessment. *Early Education, 19,* 3–5.

Hall, N. (1987). *The emergence of literacy.* Sevenoaks, UK: Hodder and Stoughton.

Hall, N. (1991). Play and the emergence of literacy. In J.F. Christie (Ed.), *Play and early literacy development.* Albany, NY: State University of New York Press.

Hannon, P., & James, S. (1990). Parents' and teachers' perspectives on pre-school literacy development. *British Educational Research Journal, 16*(3), 259–272.

Harste, J.C., Woodward, V.A., & Burke, C.L. (1984). *Language stories and literacy lessons.* Portsmouth, NH: Heinemann.

Heath, S.B. (1982). What no bedtime story means: Narrative skills at home and at school. *Language in Society, 11,* 49–75.

Hiebert, E.H. (1978). Pre-school children's understanding of written language. *Child Development, 49,* 1231–1234.

Kirkland, L., Aldridge, J., & Kuby, P. (1991). Environmental print and the kindergarten classroom. *Reading Improvement, 28,* 219–222.

Kuby, P., Aldridge, J., & Snyder, S. (1994). Developmental progression of environmental print recognition in kindergarten children. *Reading Psychology, 15,* 1–9.

Kumar, V. (1993). *Poverty and inequality in the U.K.: The effects on children.* London: National Children's Bureau.

Laminack, L.L. (1991). *Learning with Zachary.* Richmond Hill, ON: Ashton Scholastic.

Lass, B. (1983). Portrait of my son as an early reader II. *The Reading Teacher, 36,* 508–515.

Leichter, H.J. (1984). Families as environments for literacy. In H. Goelman, A. Oberg, & F. Smith (Eds.), *Awakening to literacy.* London: Heinemann.

Masonheimer, P.E., Drum, P.A., & Ellis, L.C. (1984). Does environmental print identification lead children into word reading? *Journal of Reading Behavior, 16,* 257–271.

Meek, M. (1982). *Learning to read.* London: Bodley Head.

Miller, L. (1992). *A share-a-book scheme in a pre-school playgroup.* Unpublished master's thesis, University of Hertfordshire, UK.

Miller, L. (1996). *Towards reading: Literacy development in the pre-school years.* Milton Keynes, UK: Open University Press.

Minns, H. (1997). *Read it to me now* (2nd ed.). London: Virago Press

Neuman, S.B., & Roskos, K. (1993). Access to print for children of poverty: Differential effects of adult mediation and literacy enriched play settings on environmental print and functional print tasks. *American Educational Research Journal, 30*(1), 95–122.

Nutbrown, C., & Hannon, P. (1993). Assessing early literacy—new methods needed. *International Journal of Early Childhood, 25*(2), 27–30.

Payton, S. (1984). *Developing awareness of print: A young child's first steps towards literacy* (Offset Publication No. 2). University of Birmingham Educational Review, Birmingham, UK.

Phillips, G., & McNaughton, S. (1990). The practice of storybook reading to pre-school children in mainstream New Zealand families. *Reading Research Quarterly, 25,* 196–211.

Roberts, R. (1995). *Self esteem and successful early learning.* London: Hodder and Stoughton.

Strongin Dodds, L. (1994). Learning together: Programmes for parents. *Coordinate, 39,* 12–13.

Taylor, D. (1983). *Family literacy: Young children learn to read and write.* Exeter, NH: Heinemann.

Teale, W. (1986). Home background and young children's literacy development. In W. Teale & E. Sulzby (Eds.), *Emergent literacy: Writing and reading.* Norwood, NJ: Ablex.

Vygotsky, L.S. (1978). *Mind in society: The development of higher psychological processes* (M. Cole, V. John-Steiner, S. Scribner, & E. Souberman, Eds. and Trans.). Cambridge, MA: Harvard University Press. (Original work published 1934)

Vukelich, C. (1994). Effects of play interventions on young children's reading of environmental print. *Early Childhood Research Quarterly, 9,* 153–170.

Weinberger, J. (1996). *Literacy goes to school.* London: Paul Chapman.

Weinberger, J., Hannon, P., & Nutbrown, C. (1990). *Ways of working with parents to promote literacy development.* Sheffield, England: University of Sheffield, Division of Education.

8

Literacy Development of Young Children in a Multilingual Setting

Jo Ann Brewer

A Scene From One Trilingual Classroom

Kelsi, an energetic 4-year-old, signs her name on the attendance chart near the door to the classroom and then looks carefully at what she has written. She touches each letter and counts. When she is satisfied that she has included enough letters she joins her friend Mina at a table where several children are writing on small chalk boards. Mina, who also is 4, makes scribbles that have the rounded shapes and curlicues of Khmer, the language of Cambodia. Another child scribbles all over the slate in what seems to be a random pattern. Yet another child looks around the room and copies letters that can be seen on the walls and bulletin boards, but places the letters randomly on the board.

After several minutes, Kelsi puts down the board and moves to a listening station. She finds two cow puppets there and goes in search of a friend to join her in listening to the story on tape while playing with the cow puppets. The children are able to turn on the tape machine without assistance and they know to turn the pages when the signal sounds.

Another group of children is sitting on several large beanbag chairs in the library area. They have many choices of books, some in English, some in Spanish, and some in Khmer. (The Khmer books have been written by the class or by one of the teachers because there are so few materials in Khmer available for young children.) Some of the books have been dictated by the children, illustrated, and then bound with a spiral binding. In all these class books the words are in all three languages.

The teacher goes around and warns the children that circle time will begin in a few minutes so they need to finish what they are doing very soon. As they gather in the corner, the class sits on a circle of colored paper laminated and taped to the floor. The teacher then greets the class in all three languages and the children respond in all three languages. They spend a little time in sharing news of their families or of their experiences and then begin to work on a calendar. They say the name of the days of the week and months of the year in all three languages. Next they check the classroom helper chart to see who is supposed to tell about the weather. When the weather report is finished, the teacher explains the choices that are available for work time this morning. As the children make their choices and begin working, the teacher, the paraprofessional, and the volunteers move about asking questions, making suggestions, listening to the children, and supervising their play.

The children have choices that are prepared for them by the teacher and choices that are always available, such as blocks and the sand table. At one table, children can make clothing out of scraps for a puppet figure. The basic directions are given orally, but are also in print on a rebus chart that combines the written directions with pictures. For example, one step specifies "cut the material to make a dress" (a picture of a dress is substituted for the word *dress*) and so on. At the puppet theater, the teacher encourages children to create a story for the puppets and writes down what they want the puppets to say. In another part of the room, children work with magnetic letters while teachers help them select the right letters for their names. They compare their own names with the names of their friends. Teachers are close enough to the easel to record what children say about their paintings, but no child is forced to participate. In the library center, the teacher observes the book-handling skills of the children and engages them in talk about books and stories that they especially like.

After about 45 minutes the children are asked to help put away the materials and move to the circle in the corner. On this day a parent volunteer has come to read a story. On other days, the teacher selects stories that have predictable patterns. The children "read" a familiar story in unison. The teacher then introduces a new story in a Big Book format and reads it to the children. For several days, this story will be repeated and the children will be encouraged to join in the reading as much as they can.

After a short outdoor play time, the children sing a few songs. They sing songs in each of the three languages of the classroom and do accompanying motions or movements for most of the songs. Some children can ask for the songs they like by name and some can make a selection from a large collection of song posters hanging near the music area. By this time parents are arriving to pick up their children and the morning ends.

The school these 3-, 4-, and a few early 5-year-olds attend is deliberately trilingual. The class comprises 19 children; about one-half are native English speakers, one fourth are native Spanish speakers, and the final fourth are native Khmer speakers. Most of these children could speak some English when they started school. The teacher has two assistants, one who is bilingual in Spanish and the other who is bilingual in Khmer. There also are parent volunteers to help on most days.

An observer in this classroom could hardly fail to notice the literacy development of the children in the program and the planning that has gone into developing a program that honors the languages of the classroom in both oral and written forms. The research on emerging literacy validates the activities of the children in this program and guides the planning for children as they develop in their ability to use language to meet their own needs.

Emergent Literacy

Although the concept of emergent literacy may be common, it is relatively new. Many educators began teaching when reading readiness was the guiding principle in teaching young children. Teachers engaged the children in activities that were supposed to help children learn the prerequisite skills for reading such as visual discrimination, auditory discrimination, and directionality. The concept of emergent literacy helps us recognize how much children know about reading and writing before they enter school. For example, most 3-year-olds can "write" and many 2-year-olds can "read" enough to choose their favorite breakfast cereal from the shelf or pick their favorite book for a bedtime story.

Emerging literacy is defined as the child's development of knowledge about printed language that takes place before formal instruction. Generally, children from about age 2 to about age 6 are considered to be emergent readers, although older children who have not had successful reading instruction also could be considered emergent readers. Goodman (1990) wrote the following:

> All children have some knowledge about literacy as a cultural form, and they have attitudes and beliefs about literacy as a result of their developing concepts about literacy. They know the functions that written language serves, and they know who may participate in its use. Children know what reading is and in what kinds of materials reading can occur. They know who reads, where people read, what different people use reading for, and who can and cannot read. Children know what writing is and what kinds of forms writing takes. They know who writes, what people write with, and what people use writing for. (p. 116)

For years educators ignored literacy behaviors that preceded formal instruction in reading and writing and assumed that the child came to the instructional context as a blank slate. Emergent literacy as a concept recognizes the child's learning about print and how it works before any kind of formal instruction in how to read and write. In essence, we appreciate what children have learned about the written language of their environment before they come to school.

In summarizing a number of studies of early literacy, Mason and Sinha (1993) listed the following conclusions:

- Literacy emerges before children are formally taught to read.

- Literacy is defined to encompass the whole act of reading, not merely decoding.

- The child's point of view and active involvement with emerging literacy constructs is featured.

- The social setting for literacy learning is not ignored. (p. 141)

The studies cited by these authors and many others have changed the view of literacy and what it means for a child to become literate.

As an emergent reader, the child must develop some knowledge of the functions of print, establish the mind-set of a reader, establish or make firm appropriate directional habits, identify print forms, begin to build a stock of sight words, develop phonemic awareness, and learn some let-ter-sound relations. Children develop these abilities through all their ex-periences at home as well as in a school or day-care setting, but infusing opportunities for such learning throughout the school day is a crucial com-ponent of an effective program.

How Literacy Can Be Infused in the Classroom Environment

A classroom environment that encourages the emergence of literacy abilities is one in which the teacher thinks carefully about both the psy-chological and the physical environment. The psychological environ-ment must be one in which the children are free from threat and from pressure to know certain information on a schedule or at the same time as other children. It must be individually appropriate for each child. A sec-ond element of psychological safety is a teacher who understands the de-velopmental nature of learning to read and write, who expects all children to be successful at learning, and who accepts approximations in form as signs of growth, rather than a cause for remediation. Approximations are not difficult to accept when children are learning language. No parent or caregiver would demand that an infant produce the adult form of the word *water* before giving a child a drink. In reading and writing, approxima-tions may be in the form of reading what the child thinks the text says or writing in scribbles or phonetic spellings. Teachers and parents need to think about what the child knows when the child produces a form that does not match the adult model. If a child writes *ic crem*, that child knows that representing the sounds for *ice cream* requires two words, knows the correct beginning sounds for each of those words, and knows that *c* can spell the sound heard in the word *ice*. The child needs support for what has been learned, not remediation in the spelling of *ice cream*.

The physical environment of the classroom must be arranged so that children have access to materials and time to use them. Materials for writing—paper, writing instruments, and chalkboards—should be stored so that children can get them and can put them away with as little adult help as possible. Books should be stored on open-faced shelves so that children are attracted to them and can use them when they wish. The furnishings need to be comfortable for both writing and reading activities. Tables and chairs need to be close to the writing materials for children who prefer to write at a table. Other materials, such as slates, pieces of hard-surfaced board, or clipboards also should be available so that children can write in any area of the classroom. A mailbox for each child may encourage the writing of notes. Teachers can demonstrate one of the functions of print when they keep a list of classroom supplies and encourage children to add to the list themselves when supplies are needed.

A Print-Rich Environment

One of the most important environmental factors in emerging literacy is a print-rich environment. This does not simply mean hanging charts of songs and displaying books or other print materials. It means arranging an environment that is rich in meaningful print that the children actually use. For example, a teacher might have notices and announcements that the children actually need to read, or could involve the children in keeping the attendance and milk-money records so that print is not only useful, but necessary. Print-rich environments require that children actually interact with the print, not just look at it.

The environment should be print rich in that print is used for many purposes, some in which the children participate, and some in which they see the use of print demonstrated. Print rich does not mean that the teacher has labeled all the objects in the classroom with words; it means that there are rich opportunities for engaging in the literacy process—books to read, listening centers, puppet theaters, schedules, helper charts, invitations, and calendars. The children in the trilingual school discussed in this chapter not only have a print-rich environment, but have it in three languages. They see and use print throughout their daily experiences.

Play in the Emerging Literacy Classroom

Play in the classroom has intrinsic value. In other words, it is valuable in ways other than what children can learn about literacy through play experiences. Many adults have made the mistake of thinking that if young children are not engaged in play that involves literacy in some obvious way that the play has no value. Children playing develop many social/emotional, intellectual, and physical abilities. They learn to attend to a task, take turns, solve problems, and express themselves—all valuable abilities in literacy even though the link might not be obvious to the uninitiated observer.

Play, especially sociodramatic play in which children role-play, is very valuable in terms of literacy development (see Chapter 6 for further discussion on the value of play). Children involved in such play learn to pay attention to the topic at hand for longer periods of time. Children who have a broad range of experience also bring the necessary background knowledge to their reading so that it is possible to construct meaning from a text.

Engaging in play experiences certainly contributes to children's ability to write. Writing a message requires that a child select from a repertoire of symbols the ones most useful for the purpose and arrange them in a given order. Children playing are selecting and arranging in many situations; they may select the props they want and then arrange the physical setting to meet their play goals. A child at the easel may select the colors of paint needed and then arrange them so as to achieve the desired pattern. A child playing with blocks has to gauge the distance that a given block will span when bridging from one part of a structure to another. Such play contributes to the child's ability to place letters on a page and gauge the space needed for writing tasks.

More direct connections to the development of literacy can be achieved through intervention by the teacher in the children's play activity. Several studies (Christie, 1990; Neuman & Roskos, 1993; Morrow & Rand, 1991) have found that the engagement of children in literacy activities during play increases when teachers intervene by deliberately adding literacy materials to play environments and encouraging the use of such materials. For example, Christie (1990) believes that dramatic play can support the development of literacy in young children if they are provided with literacy materials to use in their play. He notes that giving children time to play is not enough; teachers also must intervene to promote literacy activities. Such intervention may take the form of thinking about what literacy materials could be added to the play areas, encouraging children to play in theme centers where literacy is a natural response to the theme, or modeling literacy behaviors in the play areas. For example, a teacher might offer ticket books to children who are playing "riding on the train," set up an office or a grocery store area where literacy would be encouraged by the nature of the theme, or invite a child to write a label for his or her block construction.

Other theme areas that involve many literacy experiences include a doctor's office, shoe store, restaurant, home (making lists, checking the *TV Guide*, reading the newspaper, and reading to babies), and post office. Neuman and Roskos (1993) used real literacy objects rather than pretend objects. For example, they used real file folders and real forms to encourage children's use of literacy. They also suggest that literacy props be evaluated in terms of whether children would have knowledge of the use of the props from their real world experience. For example, if children were familiar with the forms and clipboards used in many doctors' offices, those would be good choices for props in an office play area.

Morrow and Rand (1991) suggest that literacy materials be kept in clearly marked places, that they be changed frequently to keep interest high, that teachers model the uses of the materials as needed or suggest possible uses when appropriate, and that all levels of development be accepted. Some children will carry around a clipboard, while others may write a list that can be decoded easily. For the most positive results from literacy play, teachers must accept children whatever their developmental level.

Connections between sustained play and literacy were noted in two ways by Roskos (1988). Her observations revealed that links to literacy were found in both the story making and literacy stance of young children. Each dramatic episode was found to contain story-making elements such as setting and characters and a goal, concern, or conflict. Literacy stance was observed in more than 450 distinct reading and writing acts displayed during play. These acts were categorized into activities (such as reading books), skills (such as printing letters and words), and knowledge (of ways to use literacy in social settings).

Roskos also suggested that teachers in day care, preschool, and kindergarten do three things to help link dramatic play and literacy:

1. Create play centers that encourage symbolic play, including experimentation with literacy.
2. Convert children's pretend-play stories into language-experience charts.
3. Carefully observe children's play for indications of literacy understanding.

The children in the trilingual school used many play materials and engaged in play episodes that are related directly to literacy. Even if some children are not engaging in literacy activities at any given time, the fact that their peers are doing so is an important observation for them.

Barclay, Benelli, and Curtis (1995) summarize an appropriate environment for the development of literacy as follows:

> ...Children will have ready access to a wide variety of print materials, including books as well as manipulatives (that is, alphabet puzzles and blocks, letter tiles, magnetic letters). Storage containers, shelves, and lockers are labeled to identify contents or with children's names. (p. 27)

They continue to describe an appropriate environment for writing:

> A well-stocked and organized writing/drawing center is available, with a variety of writing instruments (for example, chalk, markers, colored pencils, crayons, paint, letter stamps) and writing surfaces (for example, paper of differing sizes, shapes, and colors; dry-erase board; casels, chalkboards). (p. 27)

Both meaningful print in the classroom and play opportunities can contribute to children's knowledge of the functions of print. Both also help children develop the mind-set of a reader. As children are involved in story-reading experiences, in using print to keep records, or in listening to stories on tape, they can develop a concept of directionality of print (or reinforce an already developed concept).

Teachers who encourage children to handle books, make selections of books that they enjoy, and treat the selection of a favorite book as important will find that these strategies strengthen the child's mind-set as a reader. These teachers also realize that "pretend reading" is important to the child's development as a reader and encourage children to read to one another or to their dolls or stuffed animals (Fresch, 1995).

Planning Specific Literacy Experiences

Teachers may want to plan more specifically to help children develop phonemic awareness, the beginnings of a sight-word vocabulary, and letter-sound relations. In our classroom for 3- and 4-year-olds, a few children were able to segment words as they attempted to write them or to recognize words that rhymed or that had matching beginning sounds. Story-reading experiences, making class books of children's dictated responses, asking children to tell about pieces of work, and calling attention to the letters used as the statements are written down all are common strategies in good early-childhood classrooms and all contribute to phonemic awareness and knowledge of letter-sound relations (Clements & Warncke, 1994; Gunn, Simmons, & Kameenui, 1996).

Phonemic Awareness

Cunningham (1988, as cited in Griffith & Olson, 1992) defines phonemic awareness as "the ability to examine language independently of meaning and to manipulate its component sounds" (p. 516). Phonemic awareness is not a skill that children either have or do not have; it is a complex behavior that develops over time. For example, children might recognize rhyming words, then develop the ability to distinguish beginning sounds, and finally be able to segment a word into its component phonemes. Phonemic awareness is best developed during children's daily interactions with print. For example, a child wanting to write a word could be asked to think about the sounds heard when the teacher says the word slowly. Children who write words that are represented by the beginning letter or who write words phonetically are demonstrating their growing understanding of the phonemes that make up our language.

Sight-Word Vocabulary

Sight-word vocabularies often begin with the child's name and the names of his or her friends. Teachers recognize that children have learned the significance of names when they find the child rearranging the helpers chart so that their name is in place for the job they want to do. Children often spontaneously begin to recognize that some names have the same beginning letters. Other sight words that are learned quickly are *The End* as the last line of dictated stories and *Love* as a closing on a card or letter. Many children also begin to recognize color words as they are on their crayons or markers.

Letter-Sound Relations

A natural development of letter-sound relations occurs as children write, as they see their own words recorded by the teacher, and as they begin to make the association between the words on the pages of their favorite books or the lyrics to their favorite songs and the sounds of those words. As children gain skill in recording what they want to say, it is easy to observe their growing knowledge of how sounds in English, Spanish, or Khmer are recorded. Observing their writing carefully and calling attention to those relations when a child is interested are the most appropriate strategies for helping young children develop their abilities to use letter-sound relations.

Conclusion

If we return to the classroom, we can see that children are engaging in print experiences in a variety of ways and that they are exposed to stories during story time, at a listening center, a puppet stage, and through their play. They also have supportive teachers who encourage them to use what they know and to celebrate their developing abilities. Teachers model and demonstrate the use of print and the strategies for getting meaning from print throughout the day. Children accept that ideas can be expressed in more than one language and that writing what one wants to say is possible in more than one way. Every child deserves to have such an environment.

References

Barclay, K., Benelli, C., & Curtis, A. (1995). Literacy begins at birth: What caregivers can learn from parents of children who read early. *Young Children, 50*(4), 24–35.

Christie, J.F. (1990). Dramatic play: A context for meaningful engagements. *The Reading Teacher, 43*, 542–545.

Clements, N.E., & Warncke, E.W. (1994). Helping literacy emerge at school for less-advantaged children. *Young Children, 49*(3), 22–26.

Cunningham, A.E. (1988). *A developmental study of instruction in phonemic awareness.* Paper presented at the annual meeting of the American Educational Research Association, New Orleans, LA.

Fresch, M.J. (1995). Self-selection of early literacy learners. *The Reading Teacher, 49*, 220–227.

Goodman, Y. (1990). Children's knowledge about literacy development: An afterword. In Y. Goodman (Ed.), *How children construct literacy: Piagetian perspectives* (pp. 115–i23). Newark, DE: International Reading Association.

Griffith, P.L., & Olson, M.W. (1992). Phonemic awareness helps beginning readers break the code. *The Reading Teacher, 45*, 516–523.

Gunn, B.K., Simmons, D.C., & Kameenui, E.J. (1996). *Emergent literacy: Curricular and instructional implications for diverse learners.* Available: http://darkwing.uore gon.edu/~ncite/reading/EmergeLitImp.html

Mason, J.M., & Sinha, S. (1993). Emerging literacy in the early childhood years: Applying a Vygotskian model of learning and development. In B. Spodek (Ed.), *Handbook of research on the education of young children* (pp. 137–150). New York: Macmillan.

Morrow, L.M., & Rand, M.K. (1991). Promoting literacy during play by designing early childhood classroom environments. *The Reading Teacher, 44*, 396–402.

Neuman, S.B., & Roskos, K.A. (1993). *Language and literacy learning in the early years.* Ft. Worth, TX: Harcourt Brace Jovanovich.

Roskos, K. (1988). Literacy at work in play. *The Reading Teacher, 41*, 562–566.

9

A Day of Literacy Learning in a Nursery Classroom

Ruby E. Campbell

AT THE TIME OF WRITING THIS CHAPTER I WAS RESPONSIBLE FOR a class of nursery children ages 3 and 4. There were 52 children who attended this nursery class in the east of London. The children were split equally between the morning and afternoon sessions. Therefore, the classroom assistant (a nursery nurse in the United Kingdom) and I had 26 children under our supervision at any one time. During the 2½ hours that each group was at the nursery, opportunities were provided for indoor and outdoor activities, play with small and large apparatus, and group play. We provided adult support and guidance whenever it seemed appropriate. However, a constant feature of my work with the children was to ensure that there were many experiences of language and literacy. In particular I wanted to facilitate the children's emerging literacy (Hall, 1987).

In the classroom we had been thinking and talking about "people who help us." That led to a good deal of language, imaginative play, painting, model making, and writing. It also suggested some of the books we should read in the classroom. While discussing the theme of firemen, one of the many stories that I read to the children was *Barn on Fire* (Amery, 1989a).

Story reading is always an important part of the class's day, because it supports the children's literacy development (see Chapters 5 and 11 for further discussion on the value of story reading). Often it forms the starting or concluding point of the day, and frequently does both. On this occasion I read the book with the children at the end of a session. This usually means that they will talk about the book as they go home, think about it, use aspects of the story in their home activities, and begin to include words and phrases from the story in their oral language. During this story reading and as is often the case, the reading started with a discussion of the book's cover.

Teacher: If we look at the picture on the cover of the book, what do you think this story is going to be about?

Matthew: A house on fire.

Ben: I can see firemen with pipes.

Teacher: Do you think it's a house that people live in?

Cassie: No, it's chickens.

Harry: A place where the farmer keeps things.

Teacher: That's right—a barn, and the story is called *Barn on Fire* (pointing to the words).

I often point to the words to remind the children that not only does the picture tell the story but that the print also is used for stories. Once I started reading the story it took just two pages of text before there was a recognition of a character that had been part of an earlier story by the same author; the children already had enjoyed *The Naughty Sheep* (Amery, 1989b).

Cassie: It's Woolly the Lamb! (exclaiming with joy).

Teacher: Yes, it's about the same farm, with Mrs. Boot, Poppy, and Sam. But this is a different story.

Adam: There's Woolly.

Ben: They're mending the fence so he can't get out.

Teacher: That's right.

When the children recognize characters so enthusiastically it confirms their involvement in previously read stories and suggests an enjoyment of those stories. Their facial expressions and comments during each reading tell me daily about their love of hearing stories. Their activities and play during the rest of the day, often linked to the stories, also tell me about their interest in what they have heard. I encourage their involvement by getting them to join me in the story whenever possible, as is shown in the following story reading:

Teacher: Suddenly, *Sam smells smoke*. Can you smell?

Children: (All the children sniff and smell).

At that point in the story I simply asked a question that invited them to become part of the story. Later after reading page 8 I asked the children what we do if we need a fireman, so again I asked them a direct question. Their response was immediate:

Children: Dial 999 (which is correct in the UK). And ask for the fireman.

Teacher: Can you dial 999 now?

That question and response from the children was followed by us all pretending to pick up a phone, dial 999, and ask for the fireman. I also encouraged the children to make the siren noises of a fire engine. So, for a brief time there were many *ne na, ne na* sounds in the classroom. Story readings in my nursery classroom are often noisy and active learning events. But, I feel very comfortable with the noise and activity and the children quiet very quickly, aided by my nonverbal gestures and facial expressions. They then become listeners once more.

On this occasion after we finished reading the book we talked about parts of the story and the children's feelings toward it.

Teacher: So was it the barn that was on fire?

Harry: No, it was the sausages cooking.

Teacher: That's right, it was the campers cooking on a fire.

Harry: Like a barbecue.

Cassie: We've had a barbecue with hot dogs.

Zoe: So have I.

> Teacher: You lucky children, but you must all be careful and not touch anything hot—only grown-ups.
>
> Cassie: We might get burnt.
>
> Teacher: Yes, you have to be careful. Who can tell me what they liked about the story?
>
> Matthew: I liked the dog eating the sausages.
>
> Ben: I liked the fireman making the people all wet.
>
> Cassie: I liked seeing Woolly again.

The discussion gives the children an opportunity to make comments, to clarify their thoughts, and to express their feelings. Of course, it is not without its difficulties and I try to ensure that it is does not just become a simple question and answer session (Trelease, 1989). Usually the children's comments ensure that it does not adhere to a simple question and answer format, but instead becomes more of an extended discussion. After this day's discussion I invited the children to join with me in singing a song about putting out fires. The invitation led to unexpected outcomes as we started to explore the song:

> Teacher: It's a song called "London's Burning."
>
> Zoe: I know that song.
>
> Harry: So do I.
>
> Ben: And I do.
>
> Teacher: Perhaps you can come and help me.

At that point the children who were going to help with the song joined me facing the rest of the class in order to sing "London's Burning":

> London's Burning,
> London's Burning.
> Fetch the engine,
> Fetch the engine.
> Fire, Fire,
> Fire, Fire.
> Pour on water,
> Pour on water.

However, it was soon evident that, despite their confidence, the children did not know the words. So, I sang it again, and gradually more children took part in the singing and copied my actions, such as holding a hand to the mouth to call out "Fire, Fire" and pretending to "pour on water" with an imaginary bucket. However, it was a comment from Ben that led eventually to some clarification of the situation.

Ben: I saw London's Burning on TV.

Teacher: Are you sure, Ben? (somewhat puzzled)

Matthew: I saw it too.

Fortunately, at this point the nursery nurse came to my rescue and explained about a television soap opera program called "London's Burning." The children (and I) might have remained confused if that clarification had not been offered.

Teacher: Oh, I see. Well I wasn't thinking about that TV program. My song is about London a long time ago when the houses were made of wood and they were very close together. There were no telephones to get fire engines and they had to use buckets to "pour on water." Shall we sing it again?

London's Burning,
London's Burning....

The children left the classroom, telling the adults who had come to collect them all about the story or singing the song to them. This link with the parents is important and it ensures that some of the literacy learning from the classroom is developed further at home (Weinberger, Hannon, & Nutbrown, 1990)

Story Retellings

When the children returned the following day we started the session as a class on the mat and as soon as I made a comment about firemen one of the children wanted to remind the rest of the children about the story.

Retelling stories to the class or a group is a normal activity in the room, so I invited Adam to retell the story.

> Adam: The house where the chickens live was on fire and the fireman came and squirted all the water on the barbecue. The sausages were burning, not the chicken house. Then Rusty ate the sausages. The people got wet.

This retelling has almost enough detail to inform the reader about the nature of the story, including the false alarm about the barn's being on fire, when it actually was two campers creating a great deal of smoke on their campfire. (In the 1990s the campfire has been translated into a barbecue by the children.)

Inevitably the children asked for another reading of the story. The children like to hear stories again and again. It is not just enjoyment that they are getting from these readings; they also are getting new meanings with each reading, learning more new words, and acquiring new patterns of language. I seldom read a story to the class on only one occasion. My expectation is always that after we have enjoyed reading a story together a number of times, I will hear echoes of the story as I listen to the children at play. Furthermore, as they commit to memory parts of the story they create the possibility of reading the book on their own in the library corner—even though they may not look at the print during those readings.

The starting point for the second day was another reading of *Barn on Fire*, which had been brought about by the children's interest in the story from the reading on the previous day. Inevitably the story reading was interactive once again (Dombey, 1988), showing the children's involvement with the story. The children made comments about the story, the characters, and the events. They also told about their dogs—although none were called Rusty—and again talked about having a barbecue at home.

Not only did the children want to hear the story again but we also had to sing our new "London's Burning" song a number of times. With each singing more and more of the children joined in, and it was sung each time with greater enthusiasm and more pronounced actions. In order to extend their thinking about the events of the story it was possible to link with another song, as is shown in the following dialogue:

> Teacher: That was lovely. Who can remember a song about 10 fat sausages sizzling in the pan?
>
> Anneka: They go pop and bang, and then all gone.
>
> Teacher: That's right Anneka. Now, who can help me sing this song?

An attraction of this song is that it can require numerous volunteers to act the lines. Ten children become the "sausages" who stand ready for action. Then, we also had one child with cymbals for the "pop" and another child with a drum for the "bang." All the children took part in the singing.

> Ten fat sausages sizzling in the pan,
> ten fat sausages sizzling in the pan.
> One went pop, (the cymbals clash—one child sits down)
> another went bang (beat the drum—another child sits down).
> There were eight fat sausages sizzling in the pan,
> eight fat sausages sizzling in the pan.
> One went pop, (the cymbals clash—another child sits down)
> another went bang (beat the drum—another child sits down)

Eventually all the children are sitting again—so there are no sausages left in the pan. This song linked well with the story, added some language for the children to think about, and eventually led to another activity later that day as some of the children made paper sausages, created pans from boxes, and busily cooked their dinner. It also led, incidentally, to counting up to and down from ten.

Writing After the Story Reading

Later, during the course of the class session, many of the children took the opportunity to draw a picture related to the story of *Barn on Fire* and to write about their picture. Whenever possible I asked each child to tell me about the picture. Typically each picture could be recognized without my asking, but these discussions gave the children an opportunity to describe in detail what they had drawn. At the same time they also were able to tell about the writing. Their writing was such that usually it could not be deciphered easily, but it does demonstrate their knowledge about letters and in some cases sound-letter relations (Temple, Nathan, Temple, & Burris, 1988).

The children's comments about their pictures during our discussions indicated that some had concentrated on a character or object. The descriptions that they provided included the following:

Benjamin: A fire engine.

Anneka: The fireman.

Harry: The people.

Some of the other children had tried to capture part of the action of the story in their pictures as they indicated that it was about the following:

Joanne: The lady shouts.

Joe: The fire engine came.

Ben: The fire water came from the duck's pond and put out the fire.

Silver: The dog eating sausages.

The writing that the children produced demonstrated that they were thinking carefully about the content of the writing and linking it to the story that they had enjoyed so much. For some children this writing was a line of pseudo letters; others produced a collection of conventional letters that obviously was not related to what they had told me about their writing. One of the children, Ben, produced four lines of what looked like "joined up writing" with loops, circles, and vertical lines all linked together.

Of these seven children whose drawing and writing I have commented on, four produced complete and accurate writing of their first names. The other three children also produced their names in a recognizable form with the first letter always in place and some of the other letters also present. As one might expect the children gave considerable attention to the writing of their names. In doing so they had to consider the details of print. Letter shapes, letter orientation, and the sequence of the letters all were being dealt with as the children wrote their names.

Other Activities After the Story Reading

The emergence of literacy (Hall, 1987) was evident among the children as they responded to the story and expressed their feelings and thoughts in both the pictures that they produced and the writing alongside those pictures. The daily and often more frequent story reading not only captures the children's interest, it also provides a springboard to many of the other daily activities that engage the children's interest. The story provides a focus for drawing, writing, model making, play, and talk. Some of these activities were noted throughout the time of this class session after the children had listened to the story and sung the songs, in addition to their drawing and writing.

Some of the children painted full-length pictures of firemen. As they did so there were occasional bursts of

London's Burning,
London's Burning....

But, perhaps more frequently the children's emphasis was on the following lines:

Fire, fire,
fire, fire.
Pour on water,
pour on water.

Other children attempted to build model fire engines with large boxes. These attempts were quite successful because the box always can be transformed into whatever the child wants it be. Less successful were the attempts to build ladders from some of the smaller boxes—especially when children then tried to climb those ladders!

Some of the children preferred to work with play dough, which meant that they could produce not only their modeled fire engine but also firemen, the barn, and sausages in a pan. All the time during their use of play dough many of the elements of conversation that I heard seemed to link with the story that they had listened to. Some of their comments were as follows:

Matthew: My fire engine's getting water from the pond.
Cassie: I can make a hose pipe.

Ben: Ne na, ne na.
Anneka: I've got three sausages in a pan.

In the role play area children searched for dressing-up clothes that would help them become firemen and firewomen. Helmets, of course, were ideal to complete the transformation. Inevitably the telephone was used extensively and 999 was called most frequently. Interestingly, the language used on the telephone often reflected the book more than the children's expected use of language. For example, I heard the comment, "Send the fire brigade please, as fast as you can." The expectation might be for the children to request the fire engine, which are the words that are used in their geographical area to refer to that vehicle, rather than the "fire brigade" which is the language of the book. Those snippets of conversation demonstrate how the children's language is supported by the use of storybooks.

The other major use of the role play area was the use of the cooker to fry sausages. Those sausages almost always were burnt in the pan. The burnt sausages of this activity were then linked by some of the children to a request for the fire brigade, as they rushed to use the telephone.

Although the role play area was dominated by frying sausages and telephoning for the fire brigade, some children had a different agenda. A few weeks earlier we had devoted some time to talking about the doctors and dentists who help us. Some of the children returned to their interest in the medical field and wrote prescriptions based on those earlier experiences. I recognized a number of letters on the prescriptions including *m*, *c*, *L*, *e*, *o*, and *s*. The children informed me of the following:

Zoe/Georgina: We've got our prescriptions.
Teacher: Have you?
Zoe: Yes.
Teacher: Where are you going to take the prescription?
Georgina: We've got to go to the chemist.
Teacher: Yes, you will have to go to the chemist. Be careful.

The children probably would have to be careful on their way to the outdoor play area. Although in normal circumstances this fenced area is perfectly safe, today there were some fast moving "fire engines" chasing around the area. There was also the language of the story and the songs: "Get the hose pipes," "Pour on water," "Ne na, ne na," and "I'm a fire engine."

In all it had been another busy class session and although I have concentrated on telling about the literacy and linked activities during the course of a single day (together with the previous day's story reading) in reality a story remains with the children for far longer than that. As we have just noted earlier, the children come back continually to aspects of a story in the following days and weeks (Fox, 1993). There were reflections of our attention to fire engines more than 2 weeks later when I noted Jordan and Ryan building a fire engine again with boxes. From time to time, shouts of "fire" and "pour on water" could be heard.

Conclusions

This chapter has been about literacy learning in a nursery classroom during the course of the day following a story reading. I have concentrated on story readings because in our nursery we spend so much time with these readings; they provide a stimulus to much that occurs during the session as well as in the days that follow. Songs and nursery rhymes are inevitably part of this follow-up, and the parents tell me frequently how amazed they are at the number of rhymes and songs that they hear their children singing that were acquired from the classroom.

The stories also are used as a foundation for the role-play activities in which the children engage, and echoes of the story are heard in the language they use as they play. The drawings, paintings, and model making of the children often reflect the stories heard and these artifacts provide a reason for adding a written note and their name. Writing is encouraged in a large variety of ways by the stories. Writing about a character or event, using the telephone message pad, and creating a prescription were among the examples that I have described.

Often, I will use the drawings produced by the children to construct a Big Book with a simple running commentary. That book then becomes a part of the library and, as might be imagined, the children enjoy "reading" their own books. So, in a sense, the circle is complete and we are back to another book with possibilities for a story reading or shared book experience (Holdaway, 1979).

The emphasis on language and literacy in my preschool classroom is deliberate because it is so important. However, this literacy learning is achieved in an atmosphere of fun, enjoyment, and involvement. Story reading is the starting point from which, in an organized classroom, the other activities can flow.

References

Dombey, H. (1988). Partners in the telling. In M. Meek & C. Mills (Eds.), *Language and literacy in the primary school*. Lewes, UK: Falmer.

Fox, C. (1993). *At the very edge of the forest: The influence of literature on storytelling by children*. London: Cassell.

Hall, N. (1987). *The emergence of literacy*. Sevenoaks, UK: Hodder and Stoughton.

Holdaway, D. (1979). *The foundations of literacy*. London: Ashton Scholastic.

Temple, C., Nathan, R., Temple, F., & Burris, N.A. (1988). *The beginnings of writing*. London: Allyn & Bacon.

Trelease, J. (1989). *The new read-aloud handbook* (2nd rev. ed.). London: Penguin Books.

Weinberger, J., Hannon, P., & Nutbrown, C. (1990). *Ways of working with parents to promote literacy development*. Sheffield, UK: University of Sheffield, Division of Education.

Children's Literature References

Amery, H. (1989a). *Barn on fire*. London: Usborne.

Amery, H. (1989b). *The naughty sheep*. London: Usborne.

10

Establishing an Alternative Kindergarten for At-Risk 5-Year-Olds

Diane A. Walworth

IN RESPONSE TO CONCERNS ABOUT ACADEMIC PREPAREDNESS of first graders at Chenowith Elementary School, an alternative kindergarten for at-risk 5-year-olds was established. This chapter is a chronicle of the changes and real experiences in a small-town school in eastern Oregon, USA. The study was not a research project or university experiment, and too few records were kept for statistical documentation. It is, however, a reflection of what can happen when teachers believe in change and value the early literacy development of children. The alternative kindergarten is managed by Title I, a federally funded program used to supplement the regular school program and allocate funds to schools with a high incidence of poverty. The alternative kindergarten began in the fall of 1994 and continues to serve an average of 30 students per year with a full-time certified teacher and two part-time assistants.

The changes involved in setting up the alternative kindergarten were not easy. The process often was messy; it had strife and discord and stalls and flaws, but it also had celebrations and successes.

The Vision

The objectives for the alternative kindergarten were twofold. The stated objective was to intervene with 5-year-olds judged to be most at risk of academic failure and put them on a track for success. In his book *Foundations of Learning*, Holdaway (1979) wrote, "What we need is a preventive system which locates children experiencing difficulty very early before accumulating failure disorders their natural learning" (p. 167). Many of the children starting school lacked a background of literacy experiences, which put them at a disadvantage from the very beginning of their school career (Healy, 1990). They were children who had not heard stories or books, who had few, if any, books in their homes, and whose families did not spend time in meaningful conversation with them. Many lacked enriching experiences such as trips to the zoo or museums or opportunities to participate in art and music activities. For too many children their primary stimulation was television and cartoons. Often their parents were disconnected from schools, many having experienced academic failure themselves. There was a clear need to fill the gap for the children and to accelerate their early learning so they would have equal opportunities for school success. There was an additional need to involve their parents in positive, meaningful experiences associated with the school that would provide them with the necessary tools to support their child's learning at home.

The unstated objective was to provide a model of early literacy instruction that also would serve to bring about change in the regular kindergarten curriculum. The regular kindergarten was based on a nonacademic "readiness" model that did not encourage children's independent exploration of reading and writing. There was a highly structured letter identification curriculum involving the "letter people," in which a single letter was the focus of the week. Children were not given opportunities to write independently or use invented spellings nor was there encouragement of reading-like behaviors or opportunities for independent interactions with books. The curriculum was teacher centered and teacher controlled.

The alternative kindergarten began with a vision and adopted a name: Entrants class. A curriculum was envisioned that "bathed children in language" (Gonzales, 1994). By "bathing" and immersing children in literacy we hoped to provide them with experiences they might have missed in early childhood. We wanted to lessen or close the gap between those children who entered school with a wealth of literacy experiences and those who entered with a paucity or none at all. We also wanted a curriculum that intentionally developed literacy strategies. After a year in the Entrants class we hoped children would have a solid awareness of print concepts, would exhibit reading and writing behaviors, know that the purpose of print is to carry a message or meaning, and be aware of print in their everyday lives. We also hoped to foster positive attitudes toward school and literacy and create an environment where children felt safe being academic risk takers (Harste, Woodward, & Burke, 1984).

A screening device was developed to identify those children most in need of an intervention program. Many ideas were borrowed from Clay's (1993) observation survey. Suggestions also were included from kindergarten teachers and first-grade teachers about the skills and knowledge that seemed to separate students who did well in the regular classroom program from those who did poorly. Several key areas were identified that would be relatively quick and easy to measure, such as letter identification, awareness of print concepts, and counting (see the selection test in Figure 1 on pages 146–148).

Second-language learners would receive high priority for inclusion in the class because school entrance is often a traumatic experience for them. Twenty percent of the school population at Chenowith speaks Spanish as their first language, indicating a distinct need.

To promote parent involvement there was a regular schedule of home visits where the Entrants teacher talked to parents about specific ways they could support their children's learning. A bilingual assistant accompanied visits to Hispanic homes. In addition, the parents were invited to attend school family nights, which provided more opportunities to create positive school experiences and strengthen the home-school connection.

The initial year, 1994–1995, was one of trial and error, but in 1995 the Western Australian literacy resource First Steps™ became the catalyst that pulled together the objectives and vision and helped develop an effective program.

Figure 1

CHENOWITH SCHOOL DISTRICT # 9

TITLE I SELECTION TEST: ENTRANTS CLASS

STUDENT'S NAME_____   DATE OF PRETEST_____
DATE OF BIRTH_____
CLASSROOM TEACHER_____   DATE OF POSTTEST_____

(Examiner must sit next to the child when administering this test)

_____ 1. How old are you? (Knows age--1 pt.)

_____ 2. Would you please write your name on this paper for me. (5 pts)

Scoring:	All letters there	1 pt
	Captial and lower case	1 pt.
	No reversals	1 pt.
	No transpositions	1 pt.
	Legible	1 pt.

_____ 3. Show me your right hand. (1 pt.)

_____ 4. Show me your left foot. (1 pt.)

_____ 5. I would like to see how far you can count. Please begin with one. (5 pts)

Scoring:	1-5	1 pt.
	6-10	1 pt.
	11-15	1 pt.
	16-20	1 pt.
	21-25	1 pt.

_____ 6. What number is this? (Teacher displays one number at a time--10 pts)
Score 1 pt. for each number identified. 5 10 0 8 3 9 4 2 7 6

_____ 7. I am going to tell you a sentence and I want you to say it back to me. (Say
each sentence only once--2 pts total)
The cat likes to drink milk.
The kids are playing.

_____ 8. Make this shape on your paper. (1 pt. for each shape correctly drawn=4pts)

(continued)

Figure 1 (continued)

Scoring: 1 Point for each shape drawn correctly. See scoring norms below.   4 Points

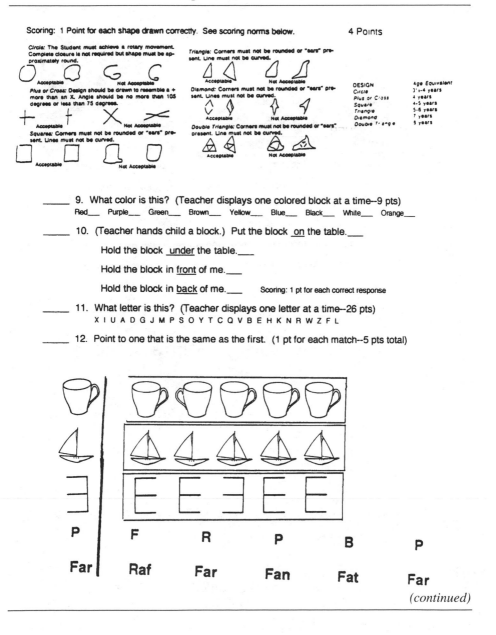

Circle: The Student must achieve a rotary movement. Complete closure is not required but shape must be approximately round.

Triangle: Corners must not be rounded or "ears" present. Line must not be curved.

Plus or Cross: Design should be drawn to resemble a + more than an X. Angle should be no more than 105 degrees or less than 75 degrees.

Diamond: Corners must not be rounded or "ears" present. Lines must not be curved.

Squares: Corners must not be rounded or "ears" present. Lines must not be curved.

Double Triangle: Corners must not be rounded or "ears" present. Line must not be curved.

DESIGN	Age Equivalent
Circle	3½-4 years
Plus or Cross	4 years
Square	4-5 years
Triangle	5-6 years
Diamond	7 years
Double Triangle	5 years

_____ 9. What color is this? (Teacher displays one colored block at a time--9 pts)
    Red___ Purple___ Green___ Brown___ Yellow___ Blue___ Black___ White___ Orange___

_____ 10. (Teacher hands child a block.) Put the block _on_ the table.___

    Hold the block _under_ the table.___

    Hold the block in _front_ of me.___

    Hold the block in _back_ of me.___   Scoring: 1 pt for each correct response

_____ 11. What letter is this? (Teacher displays one letter at a time--26 pts)
    X I U A D G J M P S O Y T C Q V B E H K N R W Z F L

_____ 12. Point to one that is the same as the first. (1 pt for each match--5 pts total)

(continued)

Figure 1 (continued)

_____ 13. Tell me about this. What does it say? (1 pt)

_____ 14. (Teacher hands the book to the child so the spine is toward the child)

Hold the book like you are going to read it to me. ___

Show me the front of the book. ___ (front cover or first page acceptable)

Show me the back of the book. ___ (back cover or last page acceptable)

scoring: 1 pt for each correct reponse

_____ 15. (Teacher opens the book to the first page of print)

If I wanted to read this to you , show me where to start reading.

_____ 16. (Teacher hands the child two blank cards.) Use these to show me one

Letter___

Word___

_____ TOTAL SCORE   80 POINTS POSSIBLE

COMMENTS:

Implementation

The first year of the alternative kindergarten program was difficult due to several contributing factors. There was a great deal of resistance toward the program from the regular kindergarten staff. They were experienced teachers who were using traditional methods and teaching lessons that they had been using for a number of years and were reluctant to change. They did not believe in teaching children to read or write before first grade or without a great deal of teacher control and supervision. During the initial year of implementation, the school schedule changed so students attended regular kindergarten full alternating days instead of traditional daily half-days. Entrants children were in regular kindergarten classes on certain days and alternative kindergarten on others. They were confused about which class they were in on any given day. Caught between two paradigms, the Entrants teacher attempted to make the transition gradually from the traditional program to the program envisioned in our Entrants objectives. However she was restricted by her limited experience with and understanding of the new model. The increased time spent in the school environment likely helped some of the Entrants children that first year, but the class did not have the expected impact.

Two things galvanized and changed the program the second year. The Entrants teacher traveled to the United Kingdom and had an opportunity to visit nursery classrooms where literacy activities were valued, encouraged, and highly evident. She saw methods to facilitate reading and writing in young children (Campbell, 1996). With a clearer vision of children's potential literacy abilities, she returned to school in the fall of 1995 eager to try new ideas. Additionally, the school adopted First Steps in 1995–1996 as a resource to help achieve literacy objectives and embarked on an intensive schedule of professional development for all teachers. Chenowith Elementary was the first school in Oregon and one of the first schools in the United States to adopt First Steps.

First Steps

First Steps is a resource developed by the Ministry of Education in Western Australia and draws from effective practices from English-speaking countries. First Steps created four developmental continua for reading, writing, spelling, and oral language that trace children's literacy development from their earliest approximations through mature mastery and control. The continua identify key behaviors children exhibit in various stages or phases of development. The key behaviors and phases of development are then linked to major teaching emphases so there is a connection between assessment and instruction. The resource books provide multiple strategies and activities to guide a teacher's instruction (see Education Department of Western Australia, 1994a, 1994b, 1994c, 1994d, 1994e).

It was apparent that there was a perfect match between the vision and objectives for the Entrants class and the philosophy and practices of First Steps. Thus First Steps became the key to the success and acceptance of the Entrants class and the focus for change in the traditional kindergarten classrooms, as well as change throughout the school.

First Steps Reading and Writing Phases

First Steps believes that from the earliest displays of reading-like or writing-like behaviors and from children's earliest experiments with reading or writing that children are in an observable and definable phase of literacy development. The model has six phases of reading development and six phases of writing development, and all phases are closely linked and intertwined. Each phase has key indicators or key significant behaviors that can be observed in children. The indicators place great importance on children's early approximations and interactions with print, and literacy is seen as an ongoing process. Both the reading and writing phases begin with the Role Play phase, which has the following key indicators. The child

- displays reading-like behavior, such as holding the book the right way up, turning the pages appropriately, looking at words and pictures, and using pictures to construct ideas;

- realizes that print carries a message but may read the writing differently each time;

- focuses on the meaning of a television program, story, or other text viewed, listened to, or "read";

- makes links to own experiences when listening to or reading books; for example, points to illustration and says, "My dog jumps up too";

- uses pictorial and visual cues when watching television or listening to or "reading" stories (talks about a television program, advertisement, or picture in a magazine or book, relating it to own knowledge and experience); and

- recognizes own name or part of it in print. (Education Department of Western Australia, 1994b).

The key indicators for the Role Play writing phase are the following. The child

- assigns a message to own symbols;
- understands that writing and drawing are different; for example, he or she points to words while "reading";
- is aware that print carries a message;
- uses known letters or approximations of letters to represent written language; and
- shows beginning awareness of directionality (that is, points to where print begins). (Education Department of Western Australia, 1994d)

As children exhibit these behaviors, the teacher highlights the indicators on an individual profile sheet. In order to accomplish this process, teachers must notice and watch what children are doing. They have to become kidwatchers (Goodman, 1991). The indicators guide the teachers' watching and make them more informed observers. At the Role Play phases, the instructional links focus largely on modeled and shared reading and modeled and shared writing. Teachers are encouraged to use Big Books, language-experience charts, environmental print, and natural contexts to demonstrate key reading and writing concepts. They also need to allow time for independent reading and writing, providing a supportive, accepting environment for children's beginning attempts at literacy. Instructional decisions are guided by where children are on the continua.

Implementation of First Steps

During the 1995–1996 school year there were approximately 30 hours of professional development to implement First Steps writing. Time was spent creating a philosophy of developmental learning and instructional practices based on problem solving, cooperative learning, and opportunities for reflecting and reporting. Teachers studied writing behaviors and placed children on the writing developmental continuum. They then began linking their instruction to student needs by using the First Steps resources. Focus shifted from what children could not do to what they could do.

In the Entrants class there was increased time devoted to modeled writing and shared writing. Each morning children were invited to participate in a written message. They looked for familiar letters in natural contexts such as the class roster, Big Books, and environmental print. Students published pattern books in both English and Spanish. Time was scheduled for independent writing and children were provided writing materials such as telephone message pads, colored paper and stationery, and greeting cards. They wrote for real purposes such as creating invitations to their parents to attend school family nights.

In the 1996–1997 school year another 30 hours of professional development was devoted to implementing First Steps reading. Teachers studied reading behaviors and learned a variety of ways to gather data about children's reading. Students were placed on the reading developmental continuum and again teachers linked instruction, this time for reading, to students' developmental phases. In the Entrants class there was a greater emphasis on modeled and shared reading, especially using informational texts. Prior to implementing First Steps, virtually all reading materials in the classroom were narrative texts. The Entrants library was expanded and students had opportunities to interact independently with predictable texts and pattern books in a variety of genres. Second-language learners received daily literacy instruction in Spanish, and an excellent selection of emergent books in Spanish were available. The children began to see themselves as readers and writers.

During the 1997–1998 school year Chenowith implemented parts of the First Steps oral language resource. First Steps oral language activities support reading and writing development. Implementation of First Steps spelling in 1998–1999 will round out and complete the literacy curriculum.

Summary

In the fall of 1996 many children who had been in the Entrants class the previous year (the first year of First Steps adoption when the most significant instructional changes occurred) were indistinguishable from their first-grade peers. All first graders were given the concepts about print

(CAP) test and letter identification test from Clay's (1993) observation survey. Former Entrants students scored an average of 13 out of 24 on the CAP test and 46 out of 54 on the letter identification test compared to 13 on the CAP and 43 on the letter identification test for non-Entrants children. These scores are important in light of their predictability of success in first grade and primary school (Adams, 1990). In addition to the test scores, the first-grade teachers reported that children who were identified in kindergarten as at risk of academic failure but who were placed in the Entrants class were better prepared for first grade than children of a similar population in the past who received no intervention. They had a positive attitude toward school and literacy and had the necessary experiences with print to scaffold continued learning.

It would seem that we have met our first objective of the Entrants program—to accelerate learning and provide background experiences in literacy for at-risk 5-year-olds. As the Entrants teacher continues to receive professional development and implements First Steps this objective is met to an increasingly greater degree.

The second objective—to influence curriculum in the traditional kindergarten classes—has been more difficult to achieve. Small but positive changes have occurred, but there still is resistance to honoring early literacy approximations and allowing independent student exploration of reading and writing. A move to viewing what children can do, rather what they cannot do, has yet to be established fully.

An alternative kindergarten that extends the time 5-year-olds spend at school and that focuses on providing literacy experiences in reading, writing, and oral language can be an effective way for schools to intervene on behalf of at-risk children and start them on a successful school career. By providing increased time spent in an enriched learning environment and by immersing children in all forms of literacy, at-risk children have an opportunity to rise to the level of their peers who enter school with a greater background of literacy experiences.

References

Adams, M.J. (1990). *Beginning to read: Thinking and learning about print (A summary)*. Urbana, IL: University of Illinois at Urbana-Champaign, Center for the Study of Reading.

Campbell, R. (1996). *Literacy in nursery education.* Stoke-on-Trent, UK: Trentham Books.

Clay, M. (1993). *An observation survey of early literacy achievement.* Portsmouth, NH: Heinemann.

Education Department of Western Australia. (1994a). *First steps oral language resource book.* Melbourne, Australia: Longman.

Education Department of Western Australia. (1994b). *First steps reading developmental continuum.* Melbourne, Australia: Longman.

Education Department of Western Australia. (1994c). *First steps reading resource book.* Melbourne, Australia: Longman.

Education Department of Western Australia. (1994d). *First steps writing developmental continuum.* Melbourne, Australia: Longman.

Education Department of Western Australia. (1994e). *First steps writing resource book.* Melbourne, Australia: Longman.

Gonzales, G. (1994, February). Presentation at the Oregon Reading Association Conference, Portland, OR.

Goodman, Y. (1991). Kidwatching. In K. Goodman, L.B. Bird, & Y. Goodman (Eds.), *The whole language catalog.* Santa Rosa, CA: American School Publishers.

Harste, J., Woodward, V., & Burke, C. (1984). *Language stories and literacy lessons.* Portsmouth, NH: Heinemann.

Healy, J. (1990). *Endangered minds.* New York: Simon & Schuster.

Holdaway, D. (1979). *The foundations of literacy.* Sydney, Australia: Ashton Scholastic.

11

To Teach or Not to Teach Reading in the Preschool... That Is the Question

Bronwyn Reynolds

A FEW YEARS AGO ONE OF MY PRESCHOOL PARENTS APPROACHED me, and out of the blue said, "Bronwyn! When are you going to teach my child to read?" As an early-childhood educator for more than 20 years, I believe this question was probably one of the most enlightened requests I have ever received. It has encouraged a deeper examination of my role as a teacher in respect to children's developing literacy. However, I admit that at the time I did not really appreciate the full implication of this remark because I considered the teaching of reading to be in the domain of the school curriculum, not that of the preschool. My reasons for this belief included a desire not to place too much pressure on the children, and a feeling that the ways of teaching initial literacy were inappropriate for very young children. (For more detail regarding the background of this philosophy refer to Reynolds, 1997.)

However, I did begin to seriously examine my philosophy on literacy in the preschool years. As a result I started to question some of my beliefs and the comments I made to parents regarding their children's developing literacy. My thoughts were reflected in questions like What should I be saying to parents with respect to the children's literacy? and How can I justify my answers to questions about literacy by talking only about prereading and prewriting skills? What really was my philosophy concerning this area of children's learning? What should I do?

After reflecting on my practice and with the knowledge that literacy does not start with formal schooling, I was presented with a challenging opportunity to explore different ways of generating emergent literacy within the preschool curriculum. The idea sounded exciting, but the thought of implementing such a program was quite daunting. Where was I to start?

Discovering Emergent Literacy

With support and guidance I set out on a journey of reading and a discovery about emergent literacy. This research heightened my thinking and understanding about how young children learn about reading and writing. I thought more about the fact that in Western cultures children are born into a print society. I pondered the fact that children do not arrive at school as empty literacy vessels waiting to be filled. Furthermore, in my quest to learn more about early literacy development, I realized my lack of constructive intervention and commitment toward developing the children's literacy in the program. Prior to any intervention the children had to rely mainly on their own experience to create contexts for literacy events in their play. Few cues or props were available to scaffold their literacy learning. (See Reynolds, 1997, for further discussion on providing cues and props in a preschool program.)

The reader may question why reference is being made to writing when the title of this chapter focuses on reading. It is very difficult to separate the two; like speaking and listening, they go together. What I have attempted to do in this chapter is to focus more on the reading side of young children's developing literacy. However, there is a large amount of overlap between reading and writing, as well as among spelling, listening, and speaking. In reality, it is quite awkward to divide these into separate subjects. They are all interrelated and have a significant effect on one another. A person cannot really write without reading. For example, how many times do you reread sentences in a letter as you write it?

We also need to consider the importance of oral communication in the development of children's emerging literacy.

Making the Literacy Environment Fun

This chapter will share how the children and I went about creating a rich literacy environment and what I did as a teacher to facilitate their learning in this area. Yet, before this discussion I want to highlight how crucial it is for learning to be fun. Remember, a wonderful recipe for success is a valued self-concept, lots of fun and praise, and a genuine interest in whatever is being undertaken currently. This pathway to success also means allowing children to pursue activities that are meaningful to them. It is very important that young children are able to use their skills and apply their knowledge by participating actively in things that make sense to them (like writing a letter to Santa or writing a sign requesting others to keep out). The major criterion here is that children enjoy learning.

Setting up a rich literate environment for preschool children may sound easy, however, I found it quite troublesome at first, especially as an early childhood educator. This is another reason I am sharing my findings with other people interested in this very important area of children's early learning. One of the first moves toward fostering a literacy enrichment program for the children was to redesign sections of the classroom. I made the following changes to the room:

- In addition to providing a large selection of books for the children, the library corner was redecorated: a fish tank, posters, signs, a tape recorder, a small felt board, magazines, comics, and newspapers all were added;
- Stories and language games on CD-ROM also became new acquisitions for the children to play with on the computer;
- Recipe books were brought in by the children and placed in the home corner, along with notepads and pencils for the children to write down their shopping lists;
- Permanent areas were allocated for numerous items, such as a large felt storyboard and a puppet theater;

• Areas of the classroom were sectioned off and depending on the children's current interest, restaurants, shopping arcades, and other businesses or community offices were constructed.

Another plan of action was to set up a writing area for the children which quickly became an office, fully equipped with a pretend computer, typewriter, stationery, writing implements, a letter box, magazines, and many books. (Refer to Reynolds, 1997, for more information on creating a literate preschool environment for children.)

I place great value in providing a range of books in the preschool program. Research now suggests that the more children are exposed to books and the earlier the exposure, the greater chance they have of being successful readers. Does this mean then that young children need to acquire certain prereading skills first, or should we encourage children's literate acts in meaningful contexts? I suggest it is the latter.

The Value of Books and Reading Aloud

Now that I have stated briefly how the power of literature can change our lives, I will discuss the power of literature in helping children become readers, without teaching them by using a "skill and drill" method. As stated previously the premise that reading to children contributes directly to their early literacy development is virtually unquestioned by researchers. We need to celebrate the fact that parents have a strong influence on their children's literacy growth. For example, Morris (1966) showed that parents who sought library membership for their children and bought books for them helped with their later reading progress.

Another project undertaken to ascertain the factors that contribute to children's progress in learning to read was conducted by Clark (1976). This study concentrated on the lives of 32 children, all of whom could read by the time they went to school at age 5. The children came from different backgrounds, ranging from the very poor to the very wealthy. However, all subjects came from families where books were read and stories were told. In commenting on the 32 fluent readers in the investigation, the important factor is that the parents themselves were avid readers and they belonged to public libraries. It also was noted that the parents all were interested in their children's development as readers and writers. Further, these parents made sure that both written and oral language were encouraged in a shared, friendly, and accepting manner.

However, it is not just reading to children that helps their literacy development, but the total environment surrounding this activity. For instance, children who have memorable experiences of parents cuddling and sharing stories with them will associate reading with pleasure. As Heath (1993) highlights in her book *Ways with Words*, what really matters is enjoying books with young children and reflecting on the books' form and content. This encourages the children's curiosity about the text and what it means and suggests that they look at the print and talk about the way the words are read. In essence, it means going beyond the world of the book. However, the vital message to be conveyed is not to leave early literacy experiences to chance, but to draw young children's awareness to different literacy acts. The crux is to weave all kinds of different literacy experiences into the children's daily lives. (Chapter 9 provides an example of the range of different literacy experiences that can be linked to the story readings of one book.)

Reading Aloud to Children Can Develop Their Vocabulary

Reading aloud to children not only helps to develop their vocabulary, but is a vital ingredient in the development of emergent reading. Book language is not the same as everyday language. For example, when I recently was reading *Wombat Divine* (Fox, 1995) to a preschool class, a 4-year-old child wanted to know what it meant when the story said, "And Wombat beamed." But before I could answer his question he replied, "It's okay I think I know the answer from the picture—He's feeling happy, isn't he?" This illustrates clearly how this young child extended his vocabulary by "reading" the picture.

Another example occurred when I was reading *Little Red Hen* (Domanska, 1974) and a 4-year-old child asked me what the word *ground* meant in this particular context. I told her and she said, "Oh that's good, now I know two different *grounds*, one for flour that you cook with and one for walking on." Teachers often assist children in this way but sometimes overlook the fact that our support as educators in these situations actually facilitates the children's learning. What we do as educators is share our knowledge with the children and provide a scaffold for their learning.

Reading Aloud Can Help Children Gain a Sense of Story

Children very quickly begin to understand narrative conversations about beginnings and endings to stories, such as, "Once upon a time," "Happily ever after," or simply "The end." They learn about prescribed roles for the different characters, like the troll in *The Three Billy Goats Gruff* (Parkes & Smith, 1986), the animals in the *Little Red Hen* (Domanska, 1974), and the fox in *The Gingerbread Man* (Parkes & Smith, 1987) and how they will act in a story.

Very quickly children begin to recognize certain story structures, such as the use of three characters in folk tales, like *The Three Bears* (Galdone, 1973), *The Three Little Pigs* (Stimson, 1993), and *The Three Billy Goats Gruff* (Parkes & Smith, 1986). For example, with the latter story children soon anticipate that if the first Billy Goat Gruff goes trip trap over the bridge, so will the second and the third. Gradually, through hearing stories read aloud, children build a schema for narrative that helps them predict the action of a story. What we also need to understand is that children gain a wonderful sense of achievement through being able to make story predictions. A delightful example of this is often captured when reading *Who Sank the Boat* (Allen, 1982), when prior to the end of the story many voices can be heard calling out, "I know, I know." Simply observing the children's expressions when they call out their answers indicates how valuable it is for children to be able to make their own predictions. What we can do in these situations is give the children a love of books as well as encourage an intrinsic motivation to explore the form and content of books.

The Importance of Rereading Stories

I also have found that children like to hear certain stories read over and over again. My own research (Reynolds, 1996) illustrates how young children enjoy revisiting their favorite stories. This may include hearing the story read aloud, "reading" the book with the use of felt character pieces, dramatizing the story with puppets (some bought and some made by the children), the children making up different versions of the story, and retelling the story from a class Big Book, written and illustrated by the children.

What has become very obvious to me is that as we examine the stories that children choose to read repeatedly, certain characteristics can be identified that assist children in reading, retelling, or memorizing stories. These characteristics include the following:

1. Language patterns or questions that are repeated throughout the story:
   Brown Bear, Brown Bear, What Do You See? by Bill Martin Jr
   I Went Walking by Sue Machin
   "Pardon?" Said the Giraffe by Colin West

2. Familiar sequence (days of the week, numbers):
   The Very Hungry Caterpillar by Eric Carle
   The Three Billy Goats Gruff retold by Brenda Parkes and Judith Smith

3. Marked story patterns with predictable plots:
   My Brown Bear Barney by Dorothy Butler
   The Chick and the Duckling by Mirra Ginsburg

4. Familiar songs and rhymes:
   The Wheels on the Bus by Maryann Kovalski
   When Goldilocks Went to the House of the Bears illustrated by Jenny Rendall

5. Cumulative stories:
   This Old Car by Colin and Jacqui Hawkins
   Who Sank the Boat by Pamela Allen

6. Easy-flap books:
   Where's Spot? by Eric Hill
   Dear Zoo by Rod Campbell

In addition to delighting the children, these stories also provide a special kind of scaffolding for learning to read.

The Power of Books

I now know as an early-childhood educator that I have underestimated the power that books can have on young children. By reading to children regularly, including the rereading of favorite stories, and encouraging them to write their own stories we are allowing them to become involved in the story. We are giving them an invitation to engage in book ideas. My research (Reynolds, 1996) indicates that many children like to gain a sense of familiarity, especially with favorite stories. By rereading stories and by appreciating and praising children's retelling of different stories we are helping them to develop into young authors. Unquestionably, in these circumstances we are facilitating the children's emerging literacy.

Becoming Authors and Illustrators

In my preschool program the children enjoy making up their own versions of different stories and they enjoy adding their names as the authors and illustrators. I also have discovered that many children like to copy particular book formats, especially those like *Brown Bear, Brown Bear, What Do You See?* (Martin, 1983) and give the story another title by using different animals and descriptions. For example, one year some of my preschoolers wrote a story based on *Brown Bear, Brown Bear*, but instead they called their book *Grey Elephant, Grey Elephant, What Do You See?*

Another example of children creating their own version of a story was with *Little Red Hen* (Domanska, 1974). A child asked me, "Why don't we have an Australian version of this story?" What a brilliant idea! I thought. So, instead of choosing a cat, dog, rat, and goose, the children collaborated and decided to include a wombat, kangaroo, koala, and kookaburra to dramatize the story.

What followed from this drama experience was the children's desire to write and illustrate their newly created version of *Little Red Hen*. This process was fascinating because I wanted the children to take responsibility for the organization of this project. After some discussion they decided that they could not spell all the words, so they nominated me as scribe. As the children dictated the story I wrote it on a piece of paper that was on my lap. However, the children were not content with this procedure, because they wanted to see how I wrote the words. So more discussion took place and it was decided that I should use an easel and a large piece of paper on which to write so that they all could see how the writing was constructed. What was really intriguing was their decision to copy the writing onto a word processor. After conferencing they also agreed to take turns typing the writing while other children nominated themselves to be the illustrators of the book. With the completion of these tasks the book was ready to be bound. We then visited the school library, where the class helped with the binding process. This book writing and illustrating activity was an absolute delight for these children and became their passion. They also gained a great deal of pleasure in being able to take home this book to show and read to members of their family.

Book Talk

Book talk also was a highlight at story time. As a group we always shared knowledge of particular books, such as the title, the author, and the illustrator. We talked about big books, little books, books with writing, and even books with no writing, for example, one particular version of the story *I Know an Old Lady* (McClelland, 1985). *Rosie's Walk* (Hutchins, 1968) was another example in which the children needed to use the illustrations to help them predict the events in the story, even though there was writing on some of the pages. As well as discussing the pictures in the book, we also focused on the writing, for example where the writing starts and which way to go when reading the print. This can be done easily in a warm and natural way by pointing to the words as the book is read aloud and involving the children as much as possible with the whole story experience.

Developing Children's Concepts of Print

The children were intrigued with different punctuation marks, such as periods, question marks, quotation marks, exclamation marks, and commas. These writing conventions were pointed out to the children in an informal and relaxed way during the reading. It became very obvious how these young children were genuinely interested in knowing about different writing conventions. Children are seekers of knowledge, so I thought it was important to involve them in the "language" of books. By including children in all types of book knowledge we are inviting them into the world of books.

Story Sharing Activities

The Book Club

Because of my obvious passion for books the children also became interested in the books I read in my leisure time. They often asked me what my favorite books were when I was a child and what they are now. Teachers should share this information with young children because it can bond together the class and teacher in what I call a "book club."

Membership in the book club also can be fostered by allocating a specific time in the program when the children can select books to look at and read to their friends. It also can be a special time for staff members, parents, grandparents, and other people to join in the program and to participate in book sharing time with the children. I found that during this period the children tended to gather around in small groups or with one friend. They found a special spot in the library area to "read" books or to listen to story tapes, or they chose to interact with stories on the computer. Setting aside times and places for using literature is another way to help children come to know the value of books.

Imitating the Reader

Another favorite book sharing activity was imitating my reading. While one child "read," another child placed the felt story pieces onto the felt board. Such interactive story processes were engaged in daily by the children. At the same time another child could be seen holding up cue cards that were made to prompt the children with various lines of repetition in particular stories. They obviously enjoyed doing this because I often observed them engaging in problem-solving exercises about who would hold up the cue cards first.

My observations of children's imitation of story reading have illuminated how the children not only mimicked my story-reading intonations, but also modeled my sitting position. Other imitations included how the book was held and the different expressions exhibited during the reading process. On one particular occasion I was very fortunate because I was observing a class and managed to capture many of these characteristics on video when a 4-year-old girl was pretending to read *The Gingerbread Man* (Parkes & Smith, 1986) just like her teacher. This child even paused during the story, looked up at the children to whom she was reading, raised her eyebrows and simultaneously mouthed with rising intonations, "Mmm mmm mmm," and after taking a deep breath said, "And that was the end of *The Gingerbread Man*." Furthermore, this child managed to create an interesting and concentrated discussion time after the story, incorporating many of her teacher's open-ended questions.

Puppetry

On other occasions the children made up different stories using puppets. This activity sometimes extended into major productions, from asking staff members to act as scribe in writing the script, to naming and decorating the puppet theater and numbering the seats for the audience. Organization skills were developed on these occasions, especially when children had to decide who was going to be the production manager, usher, narrator, and most importantly the puppeteers. The children also liked these shows to be captured on video- or audiotape because they enjoyed listening to their voices and seeing their own puppet show. Parents of the children also were entertained on occasions when these tapes were borrowed and played at home.

Poetry

Reciting poetry was another favorite activity with the children. In all my years of teaching I have never seen a group of children so excited about participating in an activity; it may have been the "magic poetry box" that created this excitement. It became obvious to me that simply flavoring poetry with a little magic to create some fun and laughter was all that was needed to encourage young children to love poetry. However, I also found that creating an interactive process with the children was another contributing factor. This particular group of children always gained a great deal of pleasure from helping me make and prepare different teaching aids, including a magic poetry box. They covered the box with specially selected black paper and decorated it beautifully with brightly colored stars. The inside contents also were chosen carefully by the children and included a magic wand, golden gloves, and a hat with iridescent sequins sewn on it. Last I added a number of my favorite poems written on cards along with an object to represent each poem; for example, a poem like "Denny the Dancing Dinosaur" was accompanied by a small replica of a dinosaur. I waved the magic wand and a child was selected to be the magician. Then the child waved the magic wand inside the magic box. The object being touched by the wand was the chosen poem to be recited. The magician held up the poetry card along with the object and the children recited the poem. These sessions were magic!

Becoming Literate Thinkers

As stated previously it is rather pointless to try to separate reading and writing. In fact Clay (1991) contends that "the first explorations of print in the preschool years may occur in writing rather than reading" (p. 108). My research (Reynolds, 1996) also suggests that the various writing experiences in which children engage form a pathway for them toward understanding the power and functions of print.

Learning Through Meaningful Contexts

Play and print were negotiated and interwoven into many areas of the children's work. For instance, children often were seen in the home area, block area, at the nature table, and even outdoors with a clipboard, paper, and pencil, engaging in literacy activities.

The writing area also became an active center for the children. In fact it was the hub to much of the children's play. Children could be seen writing notes, letters, invitations, messages, shopping lists, and signs, many of which were included in their play themes. Letters were written (often indecipherable) and some of this correspondence was posted in the children's letter box and was routinely opened and read at "mat time."

Providing a writing area and giving children opportunities to engage in other learning centers with relevant literacy materials encourages children to explore and experiment with writing. By setting up areas of interest with the children like a travel agency, news agency, or supermarket, with props including books, newspapers, brochures, paper, writing implements, a blackboard and chalk, and a typewriter and a word processor, we are encouraging children to gain a greater understanding about the functions and purposes of print in meaningful contexts.

Summary

What developed from this literacy enrichment program was a desire to articulate to other early-childhood educators and parents of preschool age children the way in which children learn to read and write. I think we need to change our traditional views on how children learn literacy and modify our methods accordingly.

We do not need to prepare children for literacy; instead we should accept and extend what they already know. We need to understand the importance of discussing literacy as a process that occurs in natural ways in meaningful contexts. In other words, we need to discuss literacy in action. Our task then is to act as providers, facilitators, and nurturers of the children's emerging literacy.

I would like to conclude this chapter with the following poem from *Best Loved Poems of the American People* (Gillilan, cited in Trelease, 1986, p. vi).

The Reading Mother

You may have tangible wealth untold:
Caskets of jewels and coffers of gold.
Richer than I you can never be—
I had a Mother who read to me.

                    by Strickland Gillilan

References

Clark, M.M. (1976). *Young fluent readers*. London: Heinemann.

Clay, M. (1991). *Becoming literate*. Portsmouth, NH: Heinemann.

Heath, S. (1993). *Ways with words: Language, life and work in communities and class-rooms*. Cambridge, UK: Cambridge University Press.

Morris, J. (1966). *Standards and progress in reading*. Slough, UK: National Foundation of Educational Research.

Reynolds, B. (1996). *The role of an early childhood educator in children's emerging literacy*. Unpublished master's thesis, University of Melbourne, Australia.

Reynolds, B. (1997). *Literacy in the pre-school: The roles of teachers and parents*. Stoke-on-Trent, UK: Trentham Books

Trelease, J. (1986). *The read-aloud handbook*. London: Penguin Books.

Children's Literature References

Allen, P. (1982). *Who sank the boat*. Melbourne, Australia: Thomas Nelson.

Butler, D. (1989). *My brown bear Barney*. New York: Greenwillow.

Campbell, Rod. (1982). *Dear zoo*. New York: Penguin Books.

Carle, E. (1969). *The very hungry caterpillar*. New York: Philomel Books.

Domanska, J. (Illustrator, 1974). *Little red hen*. London: Hamish Hamilton.

Fox, M. (1995). *Wombat divine*. Sydney, Australia: Scholastic.

Galdone, P. (Retold, 1973). *The three bears*. New York: Houghton Mifflin.

Ginsburg, M. (1972). *The chick and the duckling*. New York: Macmillan.

Hawkins, J., & Hawkins, K. (1995). *This old car*. Sydney, Australia: Orchard Books.

Hill, E. (1980). *Where's Spot?* New York: Putnam.

Hutchins, P. (1968). *Rosie's walk*. New York: Scholastic.

Kovalski, M. (1987). *The wheels on the bus*. Toronto, ON: Kids Can Press.

Machin, S. (1991). *I went walking*. Sydney, Australia: Ashton Scholastic.

Martin, B. (1983). *Brown bear, brown bear, what do you see?* New York: Holt, Rinehart and Winston.

McClelland, L. (Illustrator, 1985). *I know an old lady*. Wellington, Australia: Ashton Scholastic.

Parkes, B., & Smith, J. (Retold, 1986). *The three billy goats gruff*. Melbourne, Australia: Methuen Australia.

Parkes, B., & Smith, J. (Retold, 1987). *The gingerbread man*. Melbourne, Australia: Methuen Australia.

Rendall, J. (Illustrator, 1986). *When Goldilocks went to the house of the bears*. Gosford, Australia: Ashton Scholastic.

Stimson, J. (Retold, 1993). *The three little pigs*. Leicestershire, UK: Ladybird Books.

West, C. (1986). *"Pardon?" said the giraffe*. London: Walker Books.

12

Nursery Children as Emerging Readers and Writers

Gill Scrivens

"WHERE'S THE K, PATRICK, WHERE'S THE K?" ASKED STEPHEN (3 years, 8 months). He was watching his friend Patrick write his name from memory and had noticed that Patrick had not used the letter *K* with which Stephen was familiar because his older brother was named Kevin. This insight came from a child whose own attempt to copy his name would suggest that he had little or no knowledge of letter shapes. Yet he had absorbed a feel for the distinct features of Patrick's name and had related this to a knowledge of letter names he had presumably brought from home. His knowledge had been largely hidden until that moment.

As a teacher involved in classroom research I had become increasingly fascinated by what has been described by other researchers as emergent literacy behaviors (Hall, 1987) of children in the nursery school where I taught. I was aware that these behaviors often were hidden—deeply embedded in the context of play and interaction. Occasionally, as with Stephen, one would be given a brief insight into a child's concepts of written language, but these occasions were rarely noticed among the commotion of a typical nursery morning. Indeed, as was observed by Tizard and Hughes (1984) and by Wells in the Bristol project (1981) such behaviors are more likely to be displayed in a home setting than at nursery school.

Subsequently, as a teacher educator of university students preparing to teach children in the early years, I was concerned with the implications that changes in planning and assessment of the nursery curriculum in the United Kingdom (Department of Education and Employment, 1996) might have on children's literacy development at the nursery stage. Were models of good practice being challenged by these changes? When reflecting on and questioning practice it would seem to be essential to again look at children to discover where best they reveal the type of behavior we wish to encourage and support.

This chapter begins by reporting an empirical study in a nursery school (Scrivens, 1995a; Scrivens, 1995b). The study examines the literacy behaviors displayed by a small group of children during their interactions with one another and with the adults at the nursery school. The conclusions from the study then will be considered in light of current changes in the nursery school provision in the United Kingdom.

The Study

The school was a self-contained unit that met every morning in a small town near London. The nursery was composed of 35 children from 3 to 5 years old, and 4 permanent adults—the teacher-researcher, two nursery nurses, and a nursery assistant. There was a great deal of parental involvement and at least one parent-helper every day. The children came from a mainly middle-class area and many appeared to have had rich literacy experiences at home. Therefore, these children would not be considered typical of the general population.

The nursery at the time was organized following traditional preschool practice. The room was arranged by the adults at the beginning of the morning with a variety of equipment in various areas. The children entered at the beginning of the day and had a choice as to what area to visit; there they could work and play at will with the equipment provided. At a set time each morning the children and adults began to tidy up while children gradually came to a table for their milk and snack. Eventually everyone had 30 minutes of play outside with large playground equipment. The morning finished with a whole-group time, usually led by the teacher, when children listened to and joined in with stories and sang rhymes and songs. The only deviation from the program was during inclement weather when there was a whole-group singing, dancing, and movement time rather than outside play.

The adults in the nursery had various roles such as carer, facilitator, controller, and instructor. Principally, however, except for the teacher who frequently would work with individuals and groups of children in an instructor role, the adults most frequently assumed the roles of carer and controller. Adults did not intervene in the children's play unless there were accidents or disputes. The role of facilitator tended to be in the context of board games or craft work, when adults would need to provide a model for children. Conversations with the children tended to be related to social and emotional aspects of the children's development.

Six of the children were studied in detail by several methods in order to illuminate their hidden knowledge about written language. The nursery also was examined in relation to the type of provision available for children's literacy development in the classroom. The area that had been set up specifically to encourage the development of language and literacy was studied in detail, both in the context of being occupied by a facilitating adult and also without that support. Finally, it was realized that when the teacher acted as a researcher, her normal interactions with children were affected. The activities she had designed to encourage the development of language and literacy were not being recorded while she was observing the target children. Therefore, she kept a detailed diary to provide insights into her contribution to the nursery setting.

The aims of the study were to investigate the emergent literacy behaviors children were bringing to the nursery school and to examine closely the provision of time, materials, and adults in order to ascertain whether the nursery was indeed supporting emergent literacy.

Looking at the Children

The observation methods of target child studies used by Sylva, Roy, and Painter (1980) in the Oxford project were used. Also, samples of the children's mark making were collected, and loosely structured interviews were recorded in an attempt to deduce children's attitudes toward and perceptions of print. The study was intended to record any emergent literacy behaviors and perceptions in this group of children over a period of several weeks.

Several methods were used to illuminate the children's hidden knowledge and understanding about written language. The intention was to attempt to look beneath the surface activity and to understand the interactions and behaviors of these children. It was believed that in this way the process of emergent literacy might be revealed along with contexts that supported that process.

Six children were chosen at random. They were Sophie, age 4 years, 7 months; Steven, age 4 years, 5 months; Adam, age 4 years, 5 months; Harry, age 4 years, 3 months; Vicky, age 3 years, 10 months; and Sarah, age 3 years, 10 months. The observations were made on mornings spent tracking each child—recording what he or she was doing, for how long, and with whom—noting every time the child changed an activity or interaction. In addition, within this loosely structured observation was a 14-minute detailed study that noted behavior and interactions every 30 seconds.

The semistructured interviews were conducted after the observations and were based on a questionnaire (see Figure 1) that was designed to identify the following:

- Some of the children's perceptions about reading and the reading process; for example, What is reading? What do you think people have to do to be able to read? Show me how people read. What does it look like? Can you show me what part of this book tells the story?

- Children's attitudes toward books; for example, Do you like looking at books? What sort of books do you like?

- Children's ideas about the functions of print; for example, Will reading be useful to you? Why? Do you think it is useful for Mummy and Daddy to be able to read? Do you think they use reading for their work?

Examples of the children's mark making were collected from the target children over several weeks. The samples were analyzed in relation

Figure 1
Questionnaire

Schedule of Questions for Semistructured Interviews

1. Do you like looking at books?
2. What sort of books do you like?
3. When do you look at books?
4. With whom do you look at books?
5. What is reading?
   (Prompt: What do you think people have to do to be able to read?)

Give the child an unopened book and say:

6. Show me how people read. (Prompt: What does it look like?)
7. Can you show me what part of this book tells the story?
8. When do you think you will be able to read?
   (Prompt: How old do you think you will be?)
9. Will reading be useful to you? (If yes, Why?)
10. Do Mummy or Daddy read?
11. Do you think it is useful for Mummy and Daddy to be able to read?
12. Do you think they use reading for their work?

to what they appeared to display about the children's developing concepts of written language as described by Clay (1975).

It appeared from the target-child observations that there was a great variety in the sort of activities and interactions in which the children's emerging literacy knowledge and skills were revealed. When this evidence was put beside what was revealed from the semistructured interviews and the children's mark making, a more distinctive picture of each child's literacy profile began to emerge. Each child will be examined in turn.

Sophie (4 years, 7 months)

What was revealing about Sophie's target-child observations was that (except for self-maintaining activities such as getting dressed and story time that were about the same for all of the children and bound in the routines of the nursery) she appeared to be a child who sustained her activities at a high cognitive level most of the time. When not playing alone, she spent her time equally between interaction with one child and a small group. She also spent a great deal of time in absorbed solitary play. Apart from 5 minutes spent looking at books at the beginning of the session she engaged in only two other types of activity—one, water play (playing with jugs, funnels, and other water toys at the indoor water trough) in which she spent a large amount of time concentrating alone—and an entire hour in imaginative play at different times during the morning.

Embedded in this imaginative play was 20 minutes playing at schools (Sophie pretended to be the teacher reading a story to other children), in which she was revealed as being able to behave like a reader. When taking the role of teacher she held the book correctly, turned the pages right to left, scanned the pages left to right and top to bottom, traced her finger along the lines, and displayed pictures to the other children. When she read the story she told it accurately and used the type of language associated with stories, for example "Once upon a time...."

It appeared from her interview that she was used to sharing storybooks at home with her parents at bedtime. When asked "How do people read?" she said, "They put their finger along the line." The interview also revealed that she knew that a book's message is held in the text and that the print is read, not the pictures. However, she acknowledged that one can get clues to the story from the pictures when she said "I look at the pictures for a long time, and then I start reading."

Nevertheless, she seemed to have a limited understanding of the functions of written language. Her concept of reading as a useful activity was limited to the necessity of being able to read stories to oneself or to one's children. Thus she could see no reason for her parents to read at work. For Sophie, reading is reading aloud; she had little concept of silent reading.

Sophie's mark making, shown in Figure 2, shows a high degree of literacy knowledge and skill. Not only did she write left to right, top to bottom—thus displaying directional knowledge—but she wrote distinguishable letters. She appeared to have some knowledge of the sounds of some of these letters and was attempting to reproduce written language by combining these letters into words. She based her hypothesis of word formation first on the initial letter sounds and then on distinguishable consonant sounds. Some of the vowel sounds also were added.

Figure 2
Sophie's Mark Making

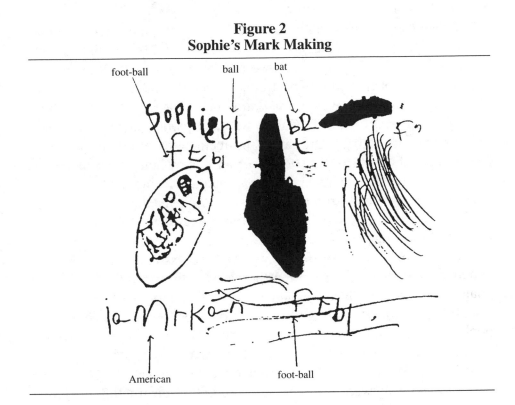

It would seem that Sophie was well on her way to being a successful reader and writer even though she had not been involved in any formal program of reading or writing instruction. This was a process that had occurred over a long period. Her writing had progressed to this stage from formless scribble when she first came to nursery a year before; several months later she had acquired the ability to write her own name. The process had occurred naturally and was probably a result of her experiences of a literate home combined with her own drive and ability to sustain concentration for long periods, to persevere at a task, and to reflect on her actions.

The high degree of interaction that she had with one other child also might be an indicator of a high cognitive level of concentration in her activities. It was found in the Oxford project that the interaction in which the highest cognitive concentration was revealed was in either a pair of children or a child and adult.

Steven (4 years, 5 months)

Conversely, Steven was revealed as having not interacted with one particular child at all on the day of his observation. Most of his interactions were spent with a group of several other boys, and a large amount of time was spent engaged in construction play with large blocks.

However, he did reveal a small amount of literacy behavior. Once again, it was during imaginary play, in which he participated with two other boys in "note taking." Dressed as policemen, they took turns scribbling on the notepad from the home corner (a play house equipped with material for role play in a home context) and delivering the "messages" to various children in the room. Here Steven displayed the knowledge that writing contains a message, as he sometimes relayed the message verbally when delivering the notes.

During his interview Steven revealed far less of an obvious commitment to literacy than Sophie. Whereas she discussed the books and reading with enthusiasm and would have given far more information than was asked for, Steven, during the discussion about books, interrupted by saying, "Yeah...and d'you know, normally...I put out a building set today...and...we got some gates there...but we haven't been able to do all of it up...and you can put cars in...to go in and out of the gates."

He obviously was far more interested in the construction play than the discussion. However, he knew that people read by "looking at the writing," and when shown a book he knew that the print told the story. When the question of usefulness of reading was discussed, Steven revealed some surprising thinking that he had presumably picked up from discussion at home. He associated learning to read with working hard, getting a job, getting rich, and thus avoiding prison. He said, "Because...the...if you didn't be able to read...you wouldn't be able to...you would land up in prison. Because...that's (not learning to read) just being naughty...you don't want to do jobs...when you're s'posed to do jobs...because then...you won't get rich."

His mark making revealed that he was at an earlier stage of development in his writing than Sophie because he could only copy his name and did not associate letters with sound (see Figure 3). However, there was some knowledge about the use of writing revealed in his imaginative play and he displayed some understanding of the relation between success in literacy and material success in life.

**Figure 3
Steven's Mark Making**

Adam (4 years, 5 months)

The most surprising thing revealed by Adam's observation was the 25 minutes when he sat in the book corner by himself and was silently absorbed in books. He was a child who appeared to spend most of his time in nursery in low intensity interactions with other children. The majority of time spent in imaginative play during the observation was made up of sporadic attempts to join in with groups of children who already were established in their play. This would often take the form of shouting and pushing other children. He gave the appearance of being hyperactive as he flitted from one activity to another. Yet, this noisy, restless child sat and looked at books slowly, deliberately, and with obvious pleasure for 25 minutes. During this time he displayed the reading behavior similar to Sophie's, as described earlier.

When interviewed, Adam displayed knowledge that reading is in the text, "not in the picture, because it hasn't got writing on it." Yet, when asked "What do people have to do to read?" he was convinced that the secret was that one had to "put on glasses and concentrate." When asked to demonstrate how it looked when a person was reading he held up his fingers to his eyes and peered through them and frowned at the page. Despite demonstrating reader-like behavior when looking at a book, getting meaning from the print was still a mystery to him.

Adam's attempt to write his name from memory was clear and neat (see Figure 4 on page 178). He was able to write some other letters and to name them. He also seemed to enjoy book making and similar activities

Figure 4
Adam's Writing

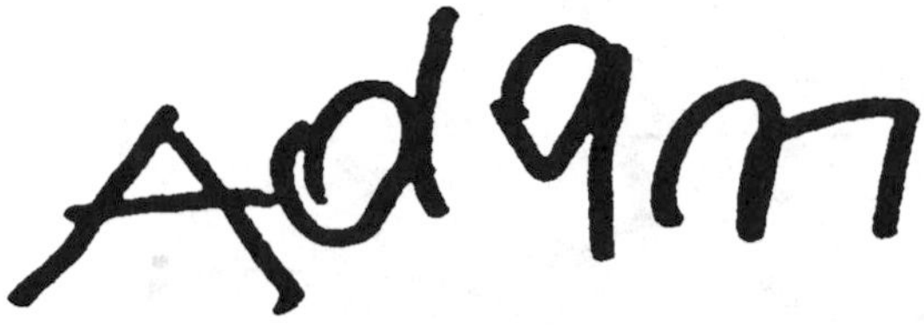

with the teacher. In certain areas, despite his often disruptive behavior, Adam was able to reveal his literacy as well as revealing a strong commitment to literary activities.

Harry (4 years, 3 months)

Harry was the most unusual child in the study. At the age of 4 years, 3 months, he was already a fluent reader. During his observation he spent 9 minutes silently reading labels on photographs that were being mounted on a display in the corridor and then telling other children what they said. However, Harry rarely chose to sit in the book corner to read. He preferred to spend most of his time either building with a group of boys or sitting by himself drawing and writing. Like Steven, Harry rarely related to just one child. During his observation morning he spent 18 minutes at the drawing and writing table. He seemed to go there when he did not know what to do next.

His writing was very neat (see Figure 5). As one would expect from a fluent reader, he had knowledge of letter shapes and he wrote some words from memory. He knew all of the letter names and sounds. However, he relied heavily on a model to copy for writing and was only just gaining the confidence to try to "work it out" on his own.

His answers in the interview revealed more knowledge and maturity than the other children displayed. When asked "What is reading?" he answered, "Well, there's words in the books and you have to read the words." He then demonstrated by subvocalizing (moving his mouth and saying the words almost silently) the beginning of the story. When asked

Figure 5
Harry's Writing

if the picture told the story at all, he said, "Well, some books you have to tell the story on yourself and there's just pictures in."

Harry was the only child who revealed mature knowledge of some of the functions of print. He said, "Because, if you have a letter, posted through the door or something... then...you've got to have someone else to read it" (if you could not read). He then talked about reading the newspaper and reading books, "because if it's got something in it that's useful to use...and if you want to buy it."

Harry revealed a great deal of knowledge and skill as a fluent reader, yet he had not had any formal instruction. He had acquired this ability during interaction with print and books in his environment and the facilitating interest of his parents, especially his mother.

Strangely, one skill he appeared less able to perform was that of oral reading. When asked if there was anything he still needed to learn about reading he said, "Well, I read in my head, but I can't really read so I can...so you can...sound me reading.... No, no, so you can hear...I can't read so you can hear me...I can only hear...I can only read in my head." Yet he could read. He often would scan print and then tell what it said.

Vicky (3 years, 10 months)

Although Vicky was observed sampling a wide variety of activities during her study morning, she engaged in nearly all of these activities with her best friend, Annie. Seventy minutes was spent exclusively with Annie.

Even when Vicky played in a group, Annie was invariably there. Once again, as noticed with Sophie who spent a large amount of time in imaginary play with one partner, there was an extended time of literary behavior embedded in the play. Vicky spent 15 minutes with Annie "pretending" to read books to her. There was also 18 minutes spent at the drawing and writing table with Annie.

During the interview Vicky showed surprisingly mature concepts about the reading process. She said, "They [people who can read] read the letters so you can hear the story." When asked to demonstrate what it looked like she opened the book and said "Mmm they read the letters off like this." Then she scanned the page like a reader and subvocalized "reader-like" language; she said, "Today, the story begins...." It was not what was in the text; she was not decoding the words but she had a good idea what the words said. She continued tracing her finger along the line of print and finished by saying "And they...right along to the end...and umm...that's how they read." She also identified several letters from her full name, Victoria.

The interview also revealed a very positive attitude toward books and reading, "because...[when you can read] you don't need Mummies and Daddies to read, and that's good.... Yeah, because you really like to read...'cos...mm...s'lovely and you can rush up high." Her parents read "'Cos they like it." These comments are an indication of the possible influence on enthusiasm for reading that can be acquired from the home environment.

Her writing was well formed and followed directional rules. She could write her full name from memory and was beginning to write other letters (see Figure 6).

Vicky saw herself as a competent person who could "almost read" and expected to be able to do so fully when she was 4 or 5 years old.

Sarah (3 years, 10 months)

The final child in the study was Sarah, who was very shy and rarely talked to adults. She had the least interaction with the teacher during the study. However, she was Sophie's best friend and spent a great deal of time in the extended imaginary play that we have already noted with Sophie. Her interview revealed little, as the teacher-researcher found it

Figure 6
Vicky's Writing

very difficult to engage Sarah in conversation. "Don't know" was the usual reply to questions, and when asked to identify the part of the book that told the story she pointed alternately to the print and then the picture.

She spent part of the morning before the interview drawing and trying to write her name from memory (see Figure 7 on page 182). Having completed the bottom line she appeared satisfied with her attempt, drew a circle around all of the print and put the writing in the "going home" tray. She had worked at this for several minutes without prompting from any adults. It was obviously important to her, because during the interview she remembered what she had done and burst out excitedly "I can...I can do my...write my name today!" This was a long speech to an adult for Sarah. It was evident from the observations of Sarah and the other young children at this nursery that there was a strong enthusiasm for writing.

During imaginary play with Sophie, Sarah also revealed surprising knowledge of the functions of print. She was observed in the home corner, "writing" on the notepad while talking and listening on the telephone. She put down the phone and, referring to the pad as though to a recipe, gathered "food" and utensils together and "cooked" a dish. She used the pad later to write a list of children to come to a party. Thus Sarah was revealing through her literacy behavior embedded in imaginary play that writing

Figure 7
Sarah's Writing

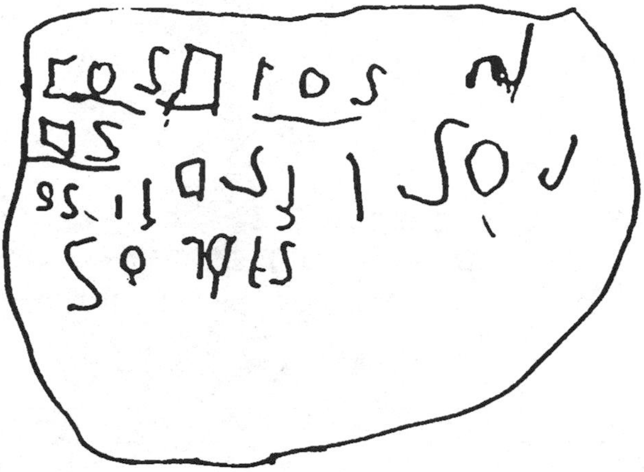

conveys a message; it can be used to record a recipe or list and it can be used as a memorandum of a discussion.

Studying the six children in this study was a most enjoyable and fascinating experience. The study indicated that these children revealed a wide range of literacy knowledge and skills that had previously gone unnoticed. In this small sample the children revealed emergent literacy behaviors during imaginary play, at the drawing and writing table, and in the book corner. Several children were able to articulate these concepts; others were less successful. Yet all revealed in their behavior, especially during imaginary play, that they would be going to primary school with a great deal more knowledge and skill than might be assumed if they were asked to perform with print in a formal setting (for example, reading flash cards, reciting letter names, or writing a sentence). They were all beginning to achieve the desirable outcomes for language and literacy demanded by the new framework for nursery education in the United Kingdom (School Curriculum & Assessment Authority, 1996).

One issue that arises from the discussion of the children is that of interaction with adults in the nursery. It is understandable that there was no interaction with the teacher during the target child observations because the teacher was behaving as a researcher during this time. However, there was very little interaction shown between the children and the other four adults in the room. The longest interaction of any sort with the adults was 17 minutes shown by Steven and this was only because an adult helped him to look for a lost toy at the end of the day.

Looking at the Language Area

Another focus for the study was the language area. Here there was a book corner and a drawing and writing table furnished with a range of seating, books, paper, pencils, and pens at which children could come and sit, look at books, and make marks.

Occasionally there would be a nursery nurse or parent-helper in the area to help when asked by the children, usually to find their name cards. Sometimes an adult would sit and read books when children asked. Occasionally the teacher would sit with certain children in the area and give instruction on letter formation and patterns. There was the feeling by nursery staff that, apart from these occasions of teacher-directed time, "just sitting with the children" might be seen as a waste of time. The professionals felt it necessary to always be busy doing something worthwhile. Therefore most of the time the area was self-sustaining and children usually worked, played, and talked without adults being present.

The language area was an obvious place to observe what children were actually doing with literacy. Hall (1987) found that writing by adults or children in nursery schools was a rare event. However, he found that when children were given opportunities for writing they demonstrated a commitment to writing and an understanding of when and why people wrote. It was hoped that observations of the language area would reveal children demonstrating commitment to writing and looking at books.

As noted previously, it was rare for an adult to be present in the area for a sustained period. However, one particular parent-helper, because she had a young baby who would sit in her push-chair or on her lap, was one adult who usually spent most of her time in the area on the mornings she helped at the nursery. It was decided to observe the area on two mornings, one when this adult was present and another morning when she was not.

Before the observation, it was intended that the children and their behavior would be the main focus. The parent-helper understood this.
Children seemed to enjoy being with this helper. However, it was not until the area observations were carried out that it was revealed just how successful she was, or what she was actually doing.

To a casual observer, the language area was well used during both
mornings. The number of children visiting the area was nearly the same on
both mornings. However, it was evident from Tables 1 and 2 that there
were significant differences in the type of activity and interaction in which
the children were engaging each morning.

When the adult was present the children would come and stay
longer—on average 26.5 minutes with the adult, as opposed to 10.5 minutes without. Yet they had the same freedom to come and go as they
pleased. When the adult was present every child who drew also tried to
write (usually his or her own name). Without the adult present five children drew and did not try to write their names or anything else. Also,
children spent far longer engaging with books when the adult was sharing the books with them than when they were looking at books alone.

Table 1
The Language Area on the Morning When a Parent-Helper Was Present

Number of children using the area	Total in minutes spent by children in the area	Average minutes spent per child in the area	Minutes drawing and writing	Minutes listening to stories with adult
19	504	26.5	265	224

Table 2
The Language Area on the Morning Without an Adult Present

Number of children using the area	Total in minutes spent by children in the area	Average minutes spent per child in the area	Minutes drawing and writing	Minutes looking at books alone or with another child
17	179	10.5	83	53

So, what sort of behavior was the parent-helper using to sustain such long commitment from children on the drawing, writing, and reading activities? The detailed observations revealed that she was not instructing in a formal sense, but was using the sort of "enabling" strategies expected in the normal behavior of an interested parent (Tough, 1976). She spent a great deal of time talking to and listening to children, watching them, providing help and materials on request, and reading to them when asked. Occasionally she would make a suggestion or focus a child on a particular aspect of something they had drawn or written. Many times she offered praise. Several times she invited children to draw, to write to, or talk to the baby. On one occasion she wrote a shopping list and answered children's questions about the shopping trip planned for that afternoon. Children were subsequently observed writing their own shopping lists. Many times she sat back and did not do anything except watch, but the children were aware of her and demonstrated how comfortable they felt in her presence by the amount of time they spent with her.

The study of the language areas was obviously on a very small scale and it would be wrong to draw too many conclusions from two observations. However, the results were surprising to the teacher-researcher and the rest of the nursery staff and deserved careful consideration. What had been perceived previously as a fairly low level activity—just sitting and talking with children in the language area—was now seen in a fresh light. The children's oral language and thinking were enhanced through sustained, meaningful conversations centered on real events with the parent-helper.

The study by Tizard and Hughes (1984) showed that whereas children often have extensive and meaningful interactions in the home while surrounded by examples of reading and writing used in everyday life, there was, with the exception of group storytelling, little support for their developing concepts of language and literacy in the nursery schools. Conversations were often short and controlling and did not engage children in problem solving or hypothesis making.

The composing and discussion of a shopping list and the children's discussion of the behavior of the baby were the kind of topics suggested by Tizard and Hughes that facilitate language development. In contrast, it could be argued that the short, activity-focused conversations normally engaged in with the professionals in other areas of the nursery might have provided inferior opportunities for the children.

The parent-helper sharing books with the children in the book corner gave the children opportunities to see her modeling book skills such as following print from left to right and top to bottom with a finger, turning the pages, focusing on a significant word, and discussing the story and pictures with individual children. Story reading to a large group, unless using Big Books, cannot always provide modeling of such skills (Campbell, 1990).

Finally, the sustained practice in drawing and mark making, combined with discussion of what the children were doing, quite possibly provided children with greater understanding of the use of writing and formation of individual letters and words than the writing patterns and letter formation activities in which the teacher usually engaged. A study by Davies (1988) suggests that children's first attempts to write their names is probably the most significant stage in early writing development and provides the most frequently used bridge from drawing into literacy. The presence of the facilitating adult certainly appeared to ensure that children were attempting to perfect this skill.

The works of Bissex (1980) and Payton (1984) give detailed accounts of their own children's developing literacy before school. They demonstrate how children form their own hypotheses about written language, often using their knowledge of spoken language and seeing the adult as a resource to be used when needed. It was just this sort of intuitive support found at home that seemed to be facilitating the children's sustained use of the language area with this particular parent-helper.

Looking at the Teacher

The teacher diary was kept only on those days when she was engaging in "normal" behavior—not on the days when observations and interviews were being carried out. The teacher simply noted the times at which each activity and interaction started and finished during five mornings, who was involved, and, when possible, some of what was said.

The diary revealed that the teacher, apart from story reading, endeavored to positively encourage language and literacy development through two major activities—book making and writing cards, on which she spent most of her time when working with the children. Both of these activities were popular with the children, who often would come and ask to be next.

It was intended in the book-making activity that every child in the class should make a book every term. These varied widely in subjects but were all based on a desire by the teacher to engage the children in longer conversations than were normal in a nursery school in order to enable the children to develop their language and to focus on some aspects of written language (Tizard & Hughes, 1984).

All of these books were made by the children and the teacher from the children's own drawings, photographs, or pictures brought from home. They encouraged extended conversations; it was quite normal for a child to have 25-minute conversations with the teacher in which a range of subjects arose from discussion of the picture that the child was using in her book. The teacher would act as a scribe for the child and write her dictated words in the book. Often older children would respond to this writing by tracing over or copying the teacher's writing. This language experience approach (Campbell, 1995) to literacy is, once again, the type of activity that a parent could initiate at home when making a scrap book.

The writing cards appear to be more like the formal type of writing exercise children might encounter at school and were perceived as such by the children. Children usually only did these in the term before they went to primary school and they were usually very keen to do them. To the children, being shown how to do the writing cards was a sign that they were big children. However, unlike primary school, because of the large ratio of adults to children it was possible for each child to do these cards individually with the teacher and have her individual attention.

The letters on each card would be looked at and talked about in relation to whether the child recognized them, for example if they were in the child's name. The letter names and sounds were discussed and the corresponding pictures looked at. Then the letters were traced over with a finger, giving attention to starting and finishing points, and traced through tracing paper with a felt pen. Finally the child would be asked to reproduce each letter without tracing but with verbal prompts from the teacher if necessary.

Most of the children handled the activity easily within their last term. Of the target children—Sophie, Steven, and Adam all had some experience with this activity before their various achievements were revealed through their target-child observations. It appeared that this activity made little difference to their ability to write or recognize letters as they all varied in their knowledge and skills. The three children who had benefited from the activity were no better or worse than the other three.

This was the only sort of formal literacy instruction that the teacher provided and it is arguable whether it helped to encourage literacy behavior any more than the assistance of the parent-helper. It is probable that it did not, because the isolated exercises were not related directly to the children's interests or needs. This activity probably was harmless and would have hindered the children's emerging literacy only if it had caused anxiety or a sense of failure.

What Can We Learn About Supporting Young Children's Literacy?

The behavior of the target children demonstrated a deep commitment to using literacy, often in the context of imaginative play, in which the literacy had a real purpose and meaning for the children. The play was not an imposed activity designed specifically to encourage literacy, but arose out of the children's own interests and concerns. Children responded to the writing materials, books, and the facilitating adult at their own levels and often played out scenarios they had witnessed at home. The drive and ability of some children to maintain sustained concentration while engaged in self-chosen literary activities seemed to be crucial to the amount of time spent and success achieved. The children were not being taught to write or read, but they were learning about literacy. (See Chapter 13 for further exploration of facilitating literacy through play.)

It would seem from this evidence that it is most important to give children of this age the freedom to move from one activity to another and to have access to plentiful materials for literacy in different areas of the room with which to practice these literacy behaviors. It might be that, if all of the areas in an early-years setting contained the materials for literacy— signs, labels, and materials for reading and writing—children would use them naturally to extend their play and, at the same time, their engagement with print.

Also, opportunity for a variety of interactional situations varying from absorbed solitary play to self-chosen pairs and groups would seem to be important. Certainly, the tendency for the girls to play in pairs was interesting and might have been linked to their greater tendency to spend time in more sedentary activities such as drawing and writing and play reading to each other. However, even Adam and Harry gained a great deal from having the freedom to sit and engage with print alone for self-chosen, extended, and uninterrupted times.

Are the current changes to nursery education in the United Kingdom opposed to suggestions described in this chapter? The document *Desirable Outcomes for Children's Learning* (School Curriculum & Assessment Authority, 1996) that states specifically what children should be able to achieve by the end of nursery education could be seen as an imposed, adult-directed curriculum. If children are to recognize letters of the alphabet by shape and sound and to write their names with appropriate use of upper and lower case letters, then direct teaching might appear to be implied. Adam's 25 minutes looking at books, Steven's notetaking as a policeman, the girls' many encounters with literacy during imaginary play, or Harry's silent reading of labels may not be recognized as being as important as that which can be checked off a list of things children should be able to achieve by the time they enter school. In addition, if under-5 settings are judged and receive funding according to whether their children achieve certain desired outcomes then there is the danger that staff will determine that children will achieve them. The facilitating approach observed in the parent-helper might be given less value than the instructing model provided by nursery staff.

It could be argued, however, that the current changes in nursery education are attempts to increase opportunity for all children. In the examples observed in the study, children came from homes where their literacy was nurtured. Adults mediated between the print in the home and community and their children. Through reading books, providing models of reading and writing, answering children's questions, and providing opportunities for children to engage with print, adults provided the foundations on which children were able to build in the nursery setting. As already noted, most of the children observed were well on their way to achieving the desirable outcomes. Not all children, however, come to nursery or their first school with these foundations. What sort of early-years setting will best nurture their literacy knowledge, understanding, and skills?

Nursery education in the United Kingdom could benefit from the adult workers reflecting on their practice and their roles, as no doubt they will in the light of proposed changes. More intentional behavior by the adults in the nursery setting could lead to more provision of opportunities for literacy than had been thought necessary before. However, there needs to be caution that, in the effort to improve provision by focusing on the skills we wish children to achieve, it is important that the nursery day does not become too structured with little time for children's self-chosen activities.

The observations of the children and the successful parent-helper in this study as well as much research over the last two decades still would suggest that, rather than imposing a teacher-directed curriculum of formal instruction for literacy, we need to build on what we know works, informed by close observation of the children.

The factors that appear to facilitate young children's literacy in the home and that can be transposed to a nursery setting are a literacy-rich environment, with time and opportunities for children to behave purposefully as readers and writers; encouragement to play, imagine, experiment, make mistakes, and ask questions; and crucially, adults who will give children time to listen to them, to model literacy for them in real situations, and to provide the materials and support that children's developing interests dictate.

References

Bissex, G. (1980). *GNYS AT WRK: A child learns to read and write*. Cambridge, MA: Harvard University Press.

Campbell, R. (1990). *Reading together*. Buckingham, UK: Open University Press.

Campbell, R. (1995). *Reading in the early years handbook*. Buckingham, UK: Open University Press.

Clay, M. (1975). *What did I write?* London: Heinemann.

Davies, A. (1988). Children's names: Bridges to literacy? *Research in Education, 40,* 19–31.

Department of Education and Employment. (1996). *Nursery education and grant-maintained schools act*. London: Her Majesty's Stationery Office.

Downing, J. (1979). *Reading and reasoning*. Edinburgh, Scotland: Chambers.

Hall, N. (1987). *The emergence of literacy*. Sevenoaks, UK: Hodder and Stoughton.

Payton, S. (1984). *Developing awareness of print: A young child's first steps toward literacy*. Birmingham, UK: University of Birmingham, Educational Faculty.

School Curriculum & Assessment Authority. (1996). *Nursery education: Desirable outcomes for children's learning on entering compulsory education*. London: Her Majesty's Stationery Office.

Scrivens, G. (1995a). "Where's the 'K' in emergent literacy?": Nursery children as readers and writers. *Early Years*, *16*(1), 14–19.

Scrivens, G. (1995b). Just sitting with the children: The adult's role in supporting literacy in nursery language area. *Early Education*, *16*, 3–5.

Sylva, K., Roy, C., & Painter, M. (1980). *Child watching in playgroup and nursery*. London: Grant and McIntyre.

Tizard, B., & Hughes, M. (1984). *Young children learning*. London: Fontana.

Tough, J. (1976). *Listening to children talking*. London: Ward Lock Educational.

Wells, G. (1981). *Learning through interaction: The study of language development*. Cambridge, UK: Cambridge University Press.

13

Facilitating Literacy Through Play and Other Child-Centered Experiences

Gretchen Owocki

YOUNG CHILDREN BRING DIVERSE KNOWLEDGE TO THEIR FIRST years of school. Some come with a framework in place for exploring written language in the ways in which it has traditionally been explored at school. They know the names of letters, they have participated in storybook reading, and they are able to write words such as *mom*, *cat*, and their own names. Other children come to school not familiar with storybooks or writing but with the print on packages from household items, recipes, television commercials, cartoons, and street signs. They may have observed family members use written language to pay bills, fill out forms, and write letters. Many children will have used a pencil and paper often, but others will have had limited access to writing materials. Some will have talked about print with their families, while others will rarely have had this kind of experience.

Play in the Preschool Setting

When children in a preschool setting have access to relevant literacy materials during play, they often read and write, making apparent their literacy knowledge. Teachers use these situations to learn about children's understandings (Whitmore & Goodman, 1995) and to help them extend their literacy-related thinking (Roskos & Neuman, 1993; Schrader, 1991). To respond effectively and creatively to children's attempts at literacy "requires teachers to focus not on teaching per se—but on the process of learning—which belongs to the child" (Schrader, 1991, p. 210). How can teachers best focus on children's processes of learning as they play? What kinds of support are facilitative of literacy learning? Although play is generally viewed as having great potential for facilitating literacy (Hall, 1991; King, 1996; Morrow & Rand, 1991; Roskos & Neuman, 1993; Schrader, 1991), many teachers do not fully understand how they can effectively use play in their classrooms and many find it difficult to explain how play promotes development in academic areas (Schrader, 1991).

On the following pages I discuss ideas for using play as a medium for facilitating literacy. I address the design of the play environment, how teachers can support literacy through play, and some of the ways in which play activities promote literacy development. I use examples from three different preschool classrooms, all located in Tucson, Arizona, USA.

Designing the Environment

To use play as a medium for facilitating literacy, it is important to fill the classroom with literacy possibilities (Neuman & Roskos, 1992). A variety of accessible reading and writing materials in the areas of the classroom where play typically occurs allows children to spontaneously use these materials as they become relevant. Such materials include all kinds of paper, markers, pencils, notebooks, storybooks, nonfiction books, maps, brochures, and pamphlets. The family living area contains packages from household items, coupons, recipes, stationery, newspapers, and magazines.

Workplace literacy centers in the classroom include the kinds of written language that children typically see in the workplace. For example, a store center could include a cash register, food packages, credit cards, checkbooks, play money, pens, coupons, receipts, and material to make shopping lists. A health center could include charts, folders, an appointment book, a scale, a yardstick, magazines, posters, and other health-related materials. Literacy centers should reflect the experiences of the children in the classroom, keeping in mind that not all children have experienced certain settings, like restaurants or travel agencies (Neuman & Roskos, 1992). The ultimate goal is to design the environment so that children can find personally meaningful ways to explore literacy materials as a part of their play.

Literacy materials are important not only because they serve as excellent play props, but also because they provide a reference point for children to discuss a variety of concepts about print (Owocki, 1995). For example, during restaurant play, children share knowledge about written language through conversations involving phrases such as, "Hey, that menu's upside down," "What does that say?" "How do you spell milk?" or "Let me write down your order." They discuss the ways in which alphabet letters are written and the ways in which words are spelled. They discuss genre and the kinds of information that might be found in a variety of written materials. They discuss their ways of interpreting these materials and the functions they serve. These conversations involve references to the physical materials of play—the menus, order pads, pencils, and chalkboards—and therefore highlight their necessity. Children have no reason to discuss a variety of literacy events without accessible materials that meet their varied needs (Wortman & Matlin-Haussler, 1989). Materials provide context for sharing and exploring information about written language.

Materials are also valuable in that they provide a concrete reference point for the use of abstract literacy terms. For example, in reference to materials, children use terms such as *copy*, *read*, *write*, *say*, *words*, *spell*, *sentence*, *pages*, *the beginning*, and *the end*. It is important that children have a working understanding of these terms because they often are used by teachers, parents, and other children as they explain, model, demonstrate, and clarify literacy concepts.

Supporting Literacy Through Play

Once the classroom environment is set for children to use written language spontaneously during play, how do teachers support their growth? One way children grow in their literacy knowledge is through play itself (Vygotsky, 1934/1978), and another is through transactions within the social environment (Delgado-Gaitan & Trueba, 1991; Dyson,

1989; Whitmore & Goodman, 1995; Taylor & Dorsey-Gaines, 1988; Teale, 1986; Wells, 1986). The focus here is on the support that teachers provide.

To learn about children's unique literacy knowledge and to discover the kinds of situations in which they are comfortable exploring this knowledge, teachers often observe children at play and play with them. Because maturation and environmental experiences differ from child-to-child, no two paths to literacy are ever the same (Whitmore & Goodman, 1995). Conscientiously facilitating literacy through play involves learning about individual children's paths and then using this information to recognize the teachable moment, and to inform instruction, curriculum, the design of the classroom, and the equipping of play areas.

As teachers play with children and observe them at play, opportunities for facilitating literacy arise naturally. Facilitation implies providing a temporary framework to support children's knowledge construction (Cazden, 1983), following the child's lead. Within the context of play, this framework takes form when a teacher makes a suggestion, helps organize or extend an idea, offers support that contributes to a child's willingness to take risks, or offers an eager ear for listening (Owocki, 1995). Facilitation does not imply that the teacher intervenes in an attempt to teach children how or what to play, and does not imply that teachers attempt to transmit concepts that they think should be mastered by a certain time. Facilitation implies that the teacher supports children as they test and refine their hypotheses about written language.

A Teacher Facilitating Literacy Through Play

Consider an example of a teacher facilitating literacy through play. Mr. Field, the teacher in a multiage (2 through 6) preschool classroom serving approximately 10 children, had been observing some of his children as they set up a store one day. He invited them to bring written language into their play by suggesting the need for a shopping list. Chloe (age 2) decided to make the list. She got a marker and a piece of paper from a nearby shelf, and began to write. Mr. Field observed Chloe writing the list and helped her extend her thinking by saying, "I'm going to go to the store and buy something. Bring the list, Chloe." Mr. Field and Chloe then went to the store. Chloe handed the list to Aster (age 5), the store clerk, who unfolded it and looked at Chloe's string of alphabetic and invented characters. She said, "All right, we'll give you that." She then gave them some play food and asked, "Is this what you needed? Is that all you needed?"

Mr. Field's participation in this play event was simple enough that he could still monitor the whole classroom, yet focused enough to make a relevant suggestion. By observing before participating, he discovered a natural way in which to encourage the children to explore together a real-life function of written language. Children develop literacy because they have functional needs requiring them to read and write. Typically, understanding of function precedes control over form (Goodman, 1996). It is relevant to note that when Chloe was writing the list, she said aloud "J-F-J-F-J-Jef-J-F-Day-Def," making a mark on her paper each time she said a letter or word. It was not apparent whether she understood the concept of a shopping list. Mr. Field observed her writing but did not interrupt the play to clarify his intent. He did not say, "No, Chloe, you're supposed to be writing a shopping list"; he simply asked her to join him in going to the store.

Perhaps Mr. Field's decision not to interrupt was fortunate, because as Chloe looked on, Aster became the "teacher" by demonstrating her expectation that Chloe's list would be meaningful. She responded as if Chloe had meant to write some sort of grocery list and as if the list should contain food items. Through this event both Aster and Chloe had the opportunity to explore a function of written language within the meaningful context of play. Part of facilitating literacy through play is allowing children to learn from one another. The teacher need not do all the teaching, recognizing that children learn from exploring materials (Piaget, 1952) and from transacting with other children (Dyson, 1989; Whitmore & Goodman, 1995).

Teacher participation also can be aimed at extending or supporting literacy events that children have initiated. Consider the following two examples. In the first, Karla is at the writing table, drawing and writing in a booklet. Her writing is a combination of invented and alphabetic symbols. Mr. Field goes to where she is working and asks her about the book.

Mr. Field: What's the book about?

Karla: What animals do at night.

Mr. Field: And did you write in it too?

Karla: Yeah, on this page...This says coyotes come and howl at the moon at night when dawn is done. At morning they go into their caves...for hunters. At night. And for dawn. And this one says...

Mr. Field: This page says something different?

Karla: Yeah. It says mountain lions come and hunt their prey...

Mr. Field: Mountain lions come and hunt their prey...

Karla: Yeah, and they kill nice rabbits who are playing on good days.

Mr. Field: They kill nice rabbits who are playing on good days.

Karla: And this one says—this one has no words so I'm going to think of some words for it.

Mr. Field: Okay.

Karla: Bobcats hunt and do the same thing.

Mr. Field: Bobcats hunt and do the same thing.

Karla: But they don't have the same prey.

Mr. Field: Do you want to write that down so you can remember what it says?

Karla: No, cause each time I think I know cause I can see this [referring to the picture].

Mr. Field: Okay.

In this event, Mr. Field supports Karla in two important ways. First, he supports her literacy-related risk taking. Risk taking involves the actions of hypothesis testing and experimenting with how written language works and is an essential strategy for successful reading and writing (Harste, Burke, & Woodward, 1981). Mr. Field supports risk taking by showing his belief that Karla is capable of producing written text and that she has something meaningful to say. Children who view themselves as capable writers are the most likely to continue writing. This is not setting her up for an unpleasant surprise when she eventually discovers that her invented symbols cannot be read by others, because Karla knows she is pretending. Often, when asked what she is writing, she refers to her work in another way. She says, "I don't know yet" or "My mom needs that other kind of writing. Maybe when I'm in first grade I'll learn that kind of writing," referring to conventional writing. At this age, many children begin to recognize that there is a difference between real (conventional) and pretend (invented) writing; it is a part of their literacy development (Goodman, 1983; Owocki, 1995). Rather than using this opportunity to push Karla toward convention, Mr. Field opted to build on the child's strengths, supporting her belief that it is acceptable to take risks. There are no negative consequences for trying. He did the same for Chloe when he accepted her shopping list as valid.

Second, Mr. Field is supporting Karla in exploring a particular genre of written language. He listens as she uses oral language to talk about her pictures and her writing. Although she is not writing conventionally, she is exploring the language of exposition. Actually, the knowledge she demonstrates is quite conventional. Karla knows that some books contain factual information and she uses appropriate language forms to discuss this information.

Rosenblatt (1991) suggests that sophisticated readers bring a particular stance to each reading event. This stance influences the way that the reading is approached and therefore affects the meaning that is constructed. Karla took a predominantly efferent stance in her writing and subsequent reading by focusing on information, rather than a personal response or a story line. When readers take an aesthetic stance, they focus more on what they are seeing, feeling, and thinking; they make more personal connections than they do when they take an efferent stance. Every reading event falls somewhere along the continuum between the efferent and the aesthetic. Rosenblatt argues that mature readers are automatically able to select the appropriate stance, but that this act of "selective attention" must be learned by children. Through play, Karla is developing the ability to take stances appropriate to her reading and writing goals.

Mr. Field supports this by treating her attempt at writing as real, by expressing interest at what she has written, and by offering a suggestion for extending the event. It should be noted that Mr. Field also suggested further writing to help Karla remember what she had written. Although his suggestion was rejected, it could have led to his taking dictation, helping her organize her thoughts for more writing, or listening to her talk more about what she had written—all further possibilities for facilitating literacy. (In this example from the United States the teacher carefully facilitates the children's literacy. See examples of a mother from Australia in Chapter 2 and a teacher from the United Kingdom in Chapter 9 also facilitating preschool literacy.)

The following example further illustrates how play facilitates children's exploration of stance. A child engaged in play with a rocket ship asked Mr. Field for a newspaper. After reading it, the child announced "They're sending another rocket ship." He had set a purpose for his reading and then found the information he was seeking. The same child, during the same play event, used the language of exposition as he read from an informational book: "OK, let's read about Saturn. It's made out of gravity, and rocks and sand. Saturn's the only planet that has rings." These examples illustrate the potential for children to explore stance, a vital component of meaning construction, through their play. Of course, for this to occur, children need a reason to read. Play can provide this reason.

Taking Time for Teachable Moments

Consider an example of facilitation from another classroom, where Mrs. Sweet and an assistant teach a group of 20 four-year-olds. Mike is drawing and talking with his friends about a superhero named Jason. When he asks Mrs. Sweet how to write this name, instead of telling him she helps him construct the spelling for himself.

Mike: How do you write *Jason*?

Mrs. Sweet: What do you think it starts with?

Mike: J. (writes a J) What's the next letter?

Mrs. Sweet: What do you hear?

Mike: C (writes a C)...C. Another C? Now another C? Another C? Do I do another C?

Mrs. Sweet: What do you hear?

Mike: Son.

Mrs. Sweet: *Ja-son*. What else do you hear?

Mike: C! Does J-C-C spell *Jason*?

Mrs. Sweet: Think about it. Do you hear any other sounds? *Ja-son*.

Mike: N.

Mrs. Sweet: All right!

Mike: Does that spell *Jason*? Does this spell *Jason*?

Mrs. Sweet: Do you think it spells *Jason*?

Mike: Yes.

Mrs. Sweet: You did a great job sounding those out.

Mike: I spelled *Jason*. You spell it a *J*, a *C*, a *C*, and an *N*. That spells *Jason*.

Mrs. Sweet helped Mike focus on the key sounds in the word, but she did not do for the child what he was capable of doing on his own. He was intentionally encouraged to construct his own knowledge and to take risks. When very young children are too often supplied with spellings for words, they get the message that they should be overly concerned with standard spellings. They become afraid of taking risks, and are therefore paralyzed in their writing (Harste et al., 1981). For teachers to spend their time helping children develop strategies is well worth the effort because what children learn through one language encounter feeds a common pool of knowledge that they can draw from in subsequent language encounters (Harste et al., 1981). Over time, Mike will become more independent in such endeavors.

Facilitating Literacy Through Letter Writing

Consider a final example of a teacher facilitating literacy through play. One afternoon Bowen, Angie, and Karla had been playing king monster, queen monster, and princess monster. Mr. Field was sitting nearby occasionally observing this group, but also transacting with other children. He brought a mailbox and a brief written message to Bowen, Angie, and Karla, and said, "Pretend this is a mailbox and I have a letter for the king and queen and the princess." Although not yet reading conventionally, Karla pretended to read the note, making up content that sounded like a letter. She read, "To king monster and queen monster and the princess monster, queen of all, and prince, I would like to invite you to dinner at the All-Meat-Eaters, at once, tonight.

It so happens that Karla could be considered an expert on letter writing. Karla is a 4-year-old who understands many of the conventions of writing notes and letters and frequently writes birthday cards, holiday cards, notes to imaginary animals, notes to family members, and notes to friends. Because letters are meaningful to Karla and because she sees them as serving a function both in her real life and in her pretend play, this was a worthwhile suggestion. Letters provide familiar ground for Karla to explore various new aspects of written language. Teachers can purposefully make suggestions along the lines of individual children's areas of knowledge and interest, providing children with familiar ground on which to explore new knowledge.

Letter writing is one of many genres that Karla explores during play time at school. During my observations, she also explored fiction, the language of exposition (see example earlier), lists, computer language, restaurant language, doctor's-office language, post-office language, and more. To further explore how children develop literacy through play I focus on Karla's letter writing. Many of the principles discussed with this focus, however, are applicable to the exploration of many genres.

One morning, at a time when her father had been away on business, Karla announced that she had been "bad" during his absence and sat down to write a note to each of her parents. The note to her mother was written with a string of unconventional characters that Karla read aloud as: "I'm sorry I been acting this way." Karla put the letter into an envelope and wrote her own name on it. The note to her father said "Dear dad, I really miss you. Abbie does too. From Karla and Abbie."

How is this kind of activity facilitative of Karla's developing literacy? Although she does not yet use alphabetic symbols, Karla is exploring the kinds of language that are appropriate for a specific genre. She writes her letters in the first person. She often uses *dear* and the recipient's name to address her letters and closes by signing her name. Her letter-writing language often sounds more formal than the typical conversational language of a 4-year-old. She understands that envelopes have names on them, although she may not yet realize that it is the recipient's name that usually goes on the envelope. Perhaps this will become clear when she sends a letter through the classroom mailbox and nobody can determine the intended recipient. In a similar situation Mr. Field asked one of Karla's friends, "If you weren't here, how could I have told it was mine?"

In engaging in a variety of literacy events in her play, not only is Karla exploring genre, she is also exploring the many functions that written language serves. Letter writing itself serves many functions. The letter to her mother serves as an apology; the letter to her father serves as a declaration of affection; and the letter read during the monster play was interpreted as an invitation. As mentioned earlier, Karla also has written holiday cards, birthday cards, and notes to friends. Through these efforts she has explored the many functions that letters can serve and the kinds of language that might be appropriate for different purposes. When Karla begins to use more conventional symbols, the language of letter writing (and of her other frequently used genres) already will be in place. Karla will know what to say and how it can be expressed, freeing her to focus on and explore other concepts about print.

How is Karla's activity facilitative of her reading development? Through letter writing and reading, she is developing proficiency in constructing syntax and making meaning from text. As readers interpret text, they use their syntactic knowledge and the meaning they construct along the way to predict where the text is going and assign to it wording and sentence patterns. They do this before they actually use the visual and perceptual cues from the text to confirm or disconfirm these predictions. Readers are able to do this because they have an expectation of where the meaning is going and of the kinds of language and language patterns that will be used to express this meaning (Goodman, 1996). Karla certainly knows a lot about the language and language patterns to expect when she reads a letter. The more experience she has with interpreting different kinds of text and different genres, the more adept she will become at efficiently predicting, assigning, confirming, and disconfirming meaning as she reads from a wide variety of literature. This suggests the importance of setting up situations for children to engage in a variety of play situations in which they have reason to explore many functions and genres of written language.

Diverse Knowledge, Diverse Needs

Facilitating literacy through play and other child-centered experiences involves designing an environment in which children can use written language in a way that makes sense to them personally. Children must find the materials of play meaningful and they must find reasons for using them. A goal for many teachers is to ensure that children explore a variety of functions and genres of written language as they play and that they have materials and other children with whom to explore. The teacher recognizes that he or she is only one of the teachers in the classroom; materials and other children also are important teachers.

As teachers play with children and observe them at play, they facilitate learning by listening, by making literacy-related suggestions, by helping children organize or extend their thinking, and by treating every literacy event as real. All of this occurs following the child's lead, or the child's focus, in play. This approach is helpful in encouraging children to explore specific concepts, as well as functions and genres, of written language.

Careful observation of preschool play makes it clear that children come to school with diverse knowledge about written language. In a print-rich environment, they are able to explore this knowledge. If teachers prepare only for situations in which children can expand their knowledge in the traditional school areas (storybooks, letters and sounds, writing familiar words), they risk not learning about and building on the variety of literacy knowledge their students already have. "Only those at quite advanced levels of conceptualization can benefit from traditional instruction; they are the ones who learn what the teacher intends them to" (Ferreiro & Teberosky, 1982, p. 280).

Play is an equitable facilitator of literacy because it allows children to use and develop their varied knowledge and because it recognizes that each child's personal history is an important part of their literacy development. Teachers contribute to this equity by seeding the play environment with a wide variety of literacy materials, helping children to create meaningful contexts in which to explore these materials, and helping them further develop the knowledge they demonstrate in play.

References

Cazden, C.B. (1983). Adult assistance to language development: Scaffolds, models and direct instruction. In R.P. Parker & F.A. Davis (Eds.), *Developing literacy* (pp. 3–17). Newark, DE: International Reading Association.

Delgado-Gaitan, C., & Trueba, H. (1991). *Crossing cultural borders: Education for immigrant families in America.* New York: Falmer.

Dyson, A.H. (1989). *Multiple worlds of child writers.* New York: Teachers College Press.

Ferreiro, E., & Teberosky, A. (1982). *Literacy before schooling.* (K.G. Castro, Trans.). Portsmouth, NH: Heinemann.

Goodman, K. (1996). *On reading.* Portsmouth, NH: Heinemann.

Goodman, Y.M. (1983). Beginning reading development: Strategies and principles. In R.P. Parker & F.A. Davis (Eds.), *Developing literacy* (pp. 68–83). Newark, DE: International Reading Association.

Hall, N. (1991). Play and the emergence of literacy. In J. Christie (Ed.), *Play and early literacy development* (pp. 3–25). Albany, NY: State University of New York Press.

Harste, J., Burke, C., & Woodward, V. (1981). *Children, their language and world: Initial encounters with print* (Project NIE-G-79-0132). Washington, DC: National Institute of Education.

King, N. (1996). *Playing their part.* Portsmouth, NH: Heinemann.

Morrow, L.M., & Rand, M.K. (1991). Preparing the classroom environment to promote literacy during play. In J.F. Christie (Ed.), *Play and early literacy development*, (pp. 141–165). Albany, NY: State University of New York Press.

Neuman, S.B., & Roskos, K. (1992). Literacy objects as cultural tools: Effects on children's literacy behaviors in play. *Reading Research Quarterly, 27*(3), 203–225.

Owocki, G. (1995). *Teacher facilitation of play and emergent literacy in preschool.* Unpublished doctoral dissertation, University of Arizona, Tucson.

Piaget, J. (1952). *The construction of reality in the child.* New York: Basic Books.

Rosenblatt, L.M. (1991). The reading transaction: What for? In B.M. Power & R. Hubbard (Eds.), *Literacy in process*, (pp. 114–127). Portsmouth, NH: Heinemann.

Roskos, K., & Neuman, S.B. (1993). Descriptive observations of adults' facilitation of literacy in young children's play. *Early Childhood Research Quarterly, 8,* 77–97.

Schrader, C.T. (1991). Symbolic play: A source of meaningful engagements with writing and reading. In J.F. Christie (Ed.), *Play and early literacy development*, (pp. 189–213). Albany, NY: State University of New York Press.

Taylor, D., & Dorsey-Gaines, C. (1988). *Growing up literate: Learning from inner-city families.* Portsmouth, NH: Heinemann.

Teale, W.H. (1986). Home background and young children's literacy development. In W.H Teale & E. Sulzby (Eds.), *Emergent literacy: Writing and reading*, (pp. 173–206). Norwood, NJ: Ablex.

Vygotsky, L.S. (1978). *Mind in society: The development of higher psychological processes*. (M. Cole, V. John-Steiner, S. Scribner, & E. Souberman, Eds. & Trans.). Cambridge, MA: Harvard University Press. (Original work published 1934)

Wells, G. (1986). *The meaning makers*. Portsmouth, NH: Heinemann.

Whitmore, K., & Goodman, Y. (1995). Transforming curriculum in language and literacy. In S. Bredekamp & T. Rosegrant (Eds.), *Reaching potentials: Transforming early childhood curriculum and assessment* (145–166). Washington, DC: National Association for the Education of Young Children.

Wortman, R., & Matlin-Haussler, M. (1989). Evaluation in a classroom environment designed for whole language. In K. Goodman, Y. Goodman, & W. Hood (Eds.), *The whole language evaluation book* (pp. 45–54). Portsmouth, NH: Heinemann.

Author Index

Children's Literature Authors

Subject Index

Note: An *f* following an index entry indicates that the citation may be found in a figure, a *t* that it may be found in a table.

R

S